A History of the Banjo:

Frank Converse's Banjo Reminiscences

Edited by Paul Heller

ISBN-13: **978-1466308114**

Frank Converse and the History of the Banjo

When Frank Buchanan Converse died in 1903, his obituary, printed in newspapers throughout America, proclaimed him "The Father of the Banjo", and all noted that he was "the man who made the banjo popular and lived to see it decline in favor." Of course the instrument described in the obituary and, likely the only one known to the public in his time, was the five string variety which had been a staple of minstrel shows and an urban fascination that spawned banjo clubs on the campuses of the Ivy League, concert stage performers, and the refining influence of urban ladies and gentlemen. The obituary exaggerated the lack of popularity of "America's instrument," but the banjo did, for a time, wallow in obscurity and disfavor, only to be resurrected by the phenomenal success of country music and its dazzling progeny, bluegrass.

Born in Westfield, Massachusetts, in 1837, the musical Converse family moved to Elmira, New York, when Frank was a boy. Frank's brother Charles was later known for composing "hymns and anthems," and it was noted in a family genealogy that Frank inherited his musical ability from his father, "a musician of Puritan stock," he recalled in his "Banjo Reminiscences." The genealogy further noted of Frank, "before his time the banjo was vulgar. He made it almost classical."

A biographical sketch in the *New York Clipper* (1865) indicates that as a six year old child, Frank evinced an interest in music, studying the piano: "he is said to have been born with music on the brain." At age fourteen he discovered the charms of the banjo and, forsaking the piano (to the displeasure of his parents) he devoted every spare minute to applying the musical training he possessed to this instrument of minstrel shows and plantation slaves. He recalled that by the age of sixteen he began performing in public and soon after he joined McFarland's Minstrels, the first of many troupes, culminating in his own "company of corkers." *The Clipper* biography noted "he has worked hard to elevate and fully develop the banjo." His on-again off-again performances with various minstrel troupes were an attempt to accommodate a marriage to Harriet Maxwell and forays into the world of business. A tour of England and France with Christie's Minstrels earned him fame and a following in Europe.

Converse's memoir, serialized in *Cadenza*, a magazine for both professional musicians and aspiring virtuosos of stringed instruments, was called "Banjo Reminiscences." It appeared in 15 installments from June, 1901, through September, 1902, and comprises an idiosyncratic history of the banjo with first hand accounts of Sweeney, Emmet, Rice, Christie, and others by Converse and his cronies.

As an important primary source, the account is presented as written, and many may find Converse's language objectionable today. Racial stereotypes and epithets were used frequently in the 19th century and they are shocking and offensive. Readers should be warned that there has been no attempt to expurgate his language and its inclusion in this edition is, by no means, an endorsement or acceptance Converse's language.

The reader should also bear in mind that this is Frank Converse's version of history. It may or may not coincide with other popular or scholarly accounts. It does recount the first time he heard a banjo played, by an African-American who frequently visited Elmira with his instrument made from a gourd. He also recalls early playing styles and the performances of legendary banjoists such as Tom Briggs,

Picayune Butler, Hy Ramsey, and others. It was the playing of George Swayne Buckley, however, that made him forsake the piano for the five-stringer.

He remembers his first banjos, one of which had the skin of a neighbor's dog stretched across the rim.   A later report of Frank's banjo during his career as a performer describes it as "a sizable affair. It had a head thirteen inches in diameter, the rim was four inches deep of wooden construction and the vellum was drawn down by no less than thirty metal brackets. He said of it: 'It was a load to carry but Oh! What a tone!'"

His recollections of the development of the instrument and the makers and players of the 19th century will make fascinating reading for the modern scholar or banjo enthusiast. The extensive account of Sweeney and the addition of the fifth string is also an important contribution.

Almost from the first, he accepted students and began amassing the instructional methods that would eventually comprise his influential and erudite teaching texts. Because of his formal musical education as a piano student, Converse was well poised to write landmark works on banjo playing, and their importance cannot be overestimated in the development of instrumental technique.

There are only a handful of primary sources for this era of banjo players and minstrel shows. "Banjo Reminiscences" is essential reading for any scholar or enthusiast who relishes a first-hand look at the players and makers of the five string banjo.

Paul Heller
Barre, Vermont
September 2011

Banjo Reminiscences. I
Written Exclusively for THE CADENZA. June, 1901
BY FRANK B. CONVERSE, NEW YORK CITY.

But just entering my "teens' when first I heard a banjo, the recollection of the event is as vivid as if it were but yesterday—stronger, perhaps, than many subsequent incidents in my banjo life. There was a *something* in the sound of that banjo—crudely manipulated though it was—that gave me a delight never before experienced, and my eagerness to possess one and to play it dates from that time.

By way of introduction to these reminiscences and as furnishing a "synopsis of incidents," as it were, to which I may have occasion to refer—-though not chronologically—the following biographical sketch *which*, with portrait, appeared in the *New York Clipper* in 1865, may not be deemed inappropriate:

This celebrated teacher and performer of the banjo was born in Westfield, Mass., June 17, 1837, but his family shortly after removed to Elmira, N. Y. The Converse family were all excellent musicians, therefore the subject of our sketch may be said to have been born with music on the brain. As early as six years of age he commenced to study music, and before he had reached his twelfth birthday was an excellent player on the piano. At fourteen he first took hold of the banjo, and devoted all his spare time to the study of that instrument, applying to it theoretical musical principles, arranging a complete system of study bounded on correct musical rules acquired from his piano studies. So infatuated did he become with the old Cremona that he neglected the piano and devoted all his energies to the development of his favorite instrument. During all this time he was strenuously opposed by his parents who tried to dissuade him from his course, they thinking the banjo an instrument of but trifling consideration not susceptible to any improvement, and upon which labor and time would be foolishly thrown away; but in spite of all opposition he continued on, and, as he progressed, became more and more attached to his instrument. So rapidly did he progress that in two years he appeared for the first time in public at several amateur concerts.

Shortly after this he accepted an engagement with McFarland, then managing the Detroit theater. He took the position made vacant by the withdrawal of Hi Rumsey, who appeared between the pieces and played solos. His next engagement was with a minstrel company managed by Backus & Co., then performing at Metropolitan Hall, Chicago. This was in 1855. Remained with this troupe until it disbanded. We next find him permanently located at St. Louis, where he for some time gave lessons on the banjo. In 1856 he joined Matt. Feel's Campbell Minstrels at St. Louis, and traveled with them until the spring of 1858, visiting all the principal towns and cities in the United States, and closed with the party at what is now known as 444 Broadway, New York. He then bent his steps Southwest and stopped at Memphis, where he organized a large school and taught the banjo. After a successful season there he returned North and betook himself to Coke and Blackstone, but he was not long in finding out that he was never carved out for a limb of the law, and, after toiling over the books for six months, he returned to his old business and joined Campbell's Minstrels, then under the management of John T. Huntley, and they took a trip down through the New England States.

His next engagement was to him the most important one of his whole career. This meeting sprang into friendship, then love, followed by an elopement and marriage. He then organized a company of corkers himself, and after a successful tour he for a while retired from the stage; but he was doomed not to remain in retirement long, for he had tasted of the sweets, of traveling and the hearty plaudits of the admiring audiences. He accordingly visited Denver City, Colorado Territory, and organized a company called 'Converse and Petrie's." The next place we locate him is in San Francisco, Cal. where he was playing and teaching When he returned to this city he played a short engagement with Woods Minstrel's, at 514 Broadway, shortly after the place opened.

Mr. Converse's principal motive has been to elevate the position of his favorite instrument and its music, and has taken advantage of every opportunity to further that end, introducing it when and wherever a proper occasion offered itself, more particularly to the notice of those musicians who, through ignorance of the capabilities of the instrument, have spoken against it. On the 29th of last December these self same musicians, through appreciation of his successful efforts, tendered him a very flattering testimonial concert at Niblo's Saloon, signed by the names of all the principal music dealers and minstrel managers. The affair was a great success.

He has worked hard and done much to elevate and fully develop the banjo. He has written a complete work on the banjo for beginners, which will shortly be published by Messrs. Dick & Fitzgerald. Mr. Converse has established himself in this city as a teacher, and is really over-run with pupils, keeping all his time busily occupied; so much so that he has been compelled to obtain the assistance of Mr. Sivori, the excellent banjoist.

Mr. C. is also engaged at Wood's Minstrels, where he appears every night in one of his popular solos. He is one of the best performers on the instrument that we have ever heard.

Subsequently abandoning the stage and my professional activities and engaging in business, which finally proved uncongenial, the old longing for the footlights again possessed me and in 1866 I was off for England, where I joined the Christy's Minstrels ("Pony" George V. Moore's Company) at St. James's Hall, London, playing for an introductory solo (solos were then played standing), Yankee Doodle with variations (principally with the "thimble"), church organ imitations (executed with a very short violin bow secreted in the palm of the hand and drawn across the strings), and Trinity bell chimes on two swinging banjos; encores - selections from Il Trovatore, Sweet Home with variations, and concluding with the proper courtesy—God Save the Queen. A highly gratifying engagement, which would have been prolonged indefinitely, had not a desire to visit the continent (my intention when leaving America) dominated; for the English had shown a kindly appreciation of the banjo at my hands, and the opportunity seemed most favorable for advancing its interests.

After touring France, illness of my wife compelled my return to America. The Denver City experience mentioned in the *Clipper* article occurred in 1861, and was, I believe, the pioneer of public entertainments in that then chaotic "city" of log cabins, shanties, teepees, and a sparse scattering of hastily erected wooden buildings—the saloons, hotels and gambling houses of the embryo city, the citizens a motley, heterogeneous gathering of miners, speculators, prospectors, Mexicans, Indians, cattle drivers and roughs and toughs from "anywhere" a typical mining center, where nearly every individual, wearing conspicuously as a necessary part of his wardrobe a Navy revolver or two, often supplemented by a 'bowie" in his bootleg, was "a law unto himself," and it needed but a slight provocation to make up a case for the Coroner.

The Pike's Peak gold excitement was then at its height, and Denver the general rendezvous for the gold seekers, preparatory to starting for the diggings. At this time the idea of a railroad could hardly have been intimated; but the stampede for Denver was "on" ; the cry was "Pike's Peak or bust,' and the broad, thoroughly beaten trail leading from St. Joseph, Mo., along the Platte river was white with "Prairie Schooners"—large, heavy, freight-laden wagons, their contents protected by bow topped, white canvas coverings (hence the name), and each drawn by several yoke of oxen, urged to their utmost by their swarthy Mexican drivers, the deafening crack of whose dexterously applied short stalked whips, with heavy lashes fifteen or eighteen feet long, raising a welt where they struck, caused the poor beasts to cringe and groan even before the blow reached them.

But the schooners had company. Ox teams, mule teams, push carts, wheel barrows and all sorts of contrivances on wheels struggled along in the grand cavalcade - all making for the same goal!

Then there was the "Pony Express" that carried the mail; a daring rider on horseback racing at utmost speed and stopping barely long enough at the stations along his route to swing his mail pouch and himself on a fresh horse and be off again like a rocket. It required a man of nerve and endurance for this business, one who could either fight or outwit the Indians, who often sought to capture him.

The journey to Denver was in company with five others—Charley Petrie, an old-time minstrel and bone player, and Joe Gibbs, a fine basso, being of the party. Each contributed toward the purchase of our outfit—a yoke of oxen and a small covered wagon to carry our camp fixtures, provisions, etc., and thus equipped we joined the great procession. Frequently when camping near an Indian village, Petrie and I would go among their teepees and serenade the Indians, but I am pained to confess that while they were charmed by the bones, they were quite indifferent to the banjo. A forty days' tramp brought us to Denver.

In the peaked garret roof of one of the frame houses I have mentioned, on a rudely constructed stage, curtained at one end for a dressing room, and with rough, unplaned benches for our audience, appeared "Converse and Petrie's World Renowned Minstrels"—the members of which had been hastily recruited from the "flotsam" found drifting about the city.

Our opening was a grand success ; the house was packed and — well----
--but we gave them their moneys worth—at least so they said though perhaps it would be "different" if repeated now. But this was *then* and though encouraged to remain and grow up with the country, imperative business compelled my return to "the States" (as they expressed it), but with a feeling of satisfaction, however, in having pioneered the banjo among the Indian tribes of the plains and at Denver.

Banjo Reminiscences. II

Written Exclusively for 'THE CADENZA. July, 1901
BY FRANK B. CONVERSE, NEW YORK CITY.

To resume:

Banjo players, or those who wished to be, were not very numerous when I began, nor, in fact, were banjos either, those in the stores being poor affairs. The best were mostly home-made. I well remember my first banjo with its pine neck, rim formerly a flower sieve and the drum tacked on with brass-headed tacks. Of course, it could not be tightly drawn by this means, but then it was an easy matter to tighten it by warming it before the fire, when it would sound well until it cooled again and became slack.

My next banjo was somewhat different, really a fine toned, substantial instrument. It was made by a carpenter acquaintance; had a nicely polished cherry neck (at that time frets had not been applied to the finger-board); a peck measure cut down for the rim, and a dog skin drum obtained for me by "Jim" Wambold (a brother of Dave Wambold, who, many years later, was one of the proprietors of the San Francisco Minstrels), who took occasion one dark night to kill somebody's dog, and, removing its skin, had it prepared at a nearby tannery. Good heads were difficult to obtain in those days.

With but few exceptions it can hardly be said that at this time the instrument was played at all; mainly strummed as a characteristic accompaniment for the darkey songs of the day. Occasionally one could be met who aspired to easy jigs, walk-arounds and the like, but, generally speaking, the region above the fifth fret was a *terra incognito*. That the instrument was anything more than this didn't seem to occur to many minds, and with the musicians, or those who aspired to be thought such, it was simply frowned upon with contempt. And it is a sad reflection that, even at this day, despite the marvelous development it has shown in all that goes to make an instrument a *musical* instrument, there still exists a species with "souls so dead" that they obstinately shut their ears to fact when the banjo is in question, preferring to cherish and hug the old prejudice.

Not much like the old darkey (with whose sentiments many may acquiesce), when asked by a revivalist, "Were you not happier when you were converted than before ?" replied, "Well, sah, I'm afeered dat I took more solid comfort when I fust learned to pick de banjo." And this calls to mind another which goes to show that not alone the lowly, but the refined and cultured as well, appreciate the exhilarating qualities of our banjo.

I once was located in a Western city, where I became acquainted with a clergyman whose son I was teaching, and who invariably would enter the room when the lesson was over and insist upon my playing for him—"if only just one tune." I don't think I ever before met a person more enthusiastic and demonstrative in expressing admiration for the banjo. On one occasion, when in the very ecstasy of enthusiasm, he stopped abruptly and, assuming a most serious expression, exclaimed; "Well ——well——I do declare! (Pause.) If I wasn't a minister (pause) I—ah———I believe—I'd learn—I'd———take——lessons————myself; but——" here he stopped and, gazing at the floor, was silent. He was thinking. And it set me to thinking as well. That's all of the story; but I often recall the incident and wonder what he would have said had he gone on. Did it suddenly occur to him that at his age the undertaking was hopeless? Had he made a confession unworthy his calling and regretted it? Did he "all of a sudden" think a banjo-playing clergyman would be a scandal to his parishioners? Or to become a banjoist might necessitate a fall from grace? I wonder what *was* in his mind!

Of the banjo before "Joe" Sweeney's time, nothing authentic is recorded, and to him is accredited the construction of the instrument as it is now known. Certainly fame enough for anyone! But the claim that it was purely his invention must be accepted qualifiedly, for what may be called its prototype is seen in the gourd banjo (before mentioned), which history informs us was brought from Africa to America by the negro slaves in the days of the slave ships. Nor did it originate in Africa. To trace its germ would extend research to pre-historic times — to the time when first was heard the musical twang of the bowstring; for instruments with characteristics essentially banjo — and so, doubtless, akin to it — are included among the earliest discoveries — a fact strengthening the belief that all our stringed instruments had one common ancestry; are derived from the same common root, or germ — inspiration, if you like — and the many modifications developing throughout its evolution consistently with the taste, needs and musical requirements of the various peoples.

But why, in this family of musical instruments, the banjo should have been singled out as the one "black sheep," seems well-nigh inexplicable, other than for the senseless reason that the instrument having first domiciled with the ignorant negroes on the plantation, it necessarily must have originated there and therefore, by inference, being of so humble an origin, could possess no intrinsic musical merit. True enough, there were no players among the slaves capable of arousing its slumbering powers, and its destiny seemed fulfilled as an accompaniment to the darkey songs that told of the cotton fields, cane brakes, 'possum hunts, sweet tobacco posies, or

"Gwine to Alabama wid de banjo on my knee," etc. Isn't it remarkable that, with its home on the Southern plantation, the inherent beauties of the banjo awaited development at the hands of its white admirers in the North!

By our 'good people' it was deemed the instrument of the devil: the fancy only of a depraved mind, and sure to lead its advocates to the bad. My father, a musician of Puritan stock and a super - conscientious Presbyterian, had imbibed the prevailing prejudice, consequently the instrument was tabooed in our home, and so the stable (barn we called it then) became my only safe refuge for practice. But happily for me his prejudice, having no valid foundation, gradually subsided, and when he had become acquainted with the "devil's instrument" he experienced a change of heart.

The first banjo I ever heard was in the hands of a colored man—a bright mulatto —whose name I have forgotten. He frequently visited Elmira and the neighboring villages, playing and singing and passing his hat for collections. His *repertoire* was not very extensive, but, with his comicalities, sufficed to gain him a living. I cannot say that I learned anything from his execution, which, though amusing, was limited to the thumb and first finger, pulling or 'picking" the strings with both. He was quite conceited as to his abilities (pardonable in banjo players, I believe), and to impress his listeners with a due appreciation of them, he would announce that such a trifling circumstance as the banjo being out of tune caused him no inconvenience and so, with a seemingly careless fumbling of the pegs, he would disarrange the tuning—"fro de banjo out ' tune," he said— but merely pitching the second string a semitone higher.

This manner of fingering—as I learned in later years when visiting Southern plantations—was characteristic of the early colored player; an individual of rare occurrence, however, and whose banjo was of the rudest construction, often a divided gourd with a coon skin stretched over the larger part for the drum. With this for accompaniment he would improvise his song as he went along, generally mentioning his massa or missus or some local incident.

His fingering was unique, requiring only the first finger of the left hand for stopping the strings—on the first string at the first fret and the second string at the second fret. With the right hand he used only the first finger and thumb.

Resuming: With the next Minstrel Company which visited our town came 'Picayune' Butler, heralded as the greatest banjo player in the world, and the only acknowledged rival of the two most prominent banjoists of the period—Tom Briggs, then playing with E. P. Christy's Minstrels in New York, and "Hi" S. Rumsey, traveling with a theatrical company. As Butler's company remained in town several days, I had many opportunities for hearing him—not only in his solos, but often listening unobserved below his hotel window. As he played with the thimble, his execution—unlike anything I had ever heard, powerful and brilliant—strongly impressed me, and in my enthusiasm I thought him the most favored mortal on earth. Could I only know him, speak to him, tell him I could play "a little." But no, no too timid to intrude, I merely "hung around," playing *"hookey"* from school during his stay, hoping he might discover me—somehow.

But timidity was finally overcome and in a way most unexpected. The company performed in the Court House, the largest "hall" in the village and, as water for the wash up had to be carried in, I volunteered to assist and so gained unlimited entrée to the hall. It was Butler's custom to put his banjo in order after rehearsals for the evening performance and then run over some of his pieces. These occasions I always watched for, managing to be very busy near his dressing room—a little space screened by a curtain stretched at the rear of the stage. It happened one day while so engaged that, being eager to *see* as well as hear. I incautiously drew the curtain so far that I was discovered, whereupon the hand I was so anxious to observe was quickly raised and brought in contact with my ear with a force which nearly stunned me.

He was "awful sorry," he said; told me to come in; played a number of his pieces for me while kindly answering my many questions. He certainly had *struck* up an acquaintance with me which became more agreeable during the remainder of his stay, and enabled me to study not only his style of execution, but his principal pieces as well which, displayed upon the staff, I found were not so elaborate or difficult as they seemed when he played them. But I had gained some new ideas. Still more, I had heard a real "champion," had studied his execution, analyzed his pieces whereby he had assumed the title, and — well — I was encouraged. And now having acquired a pretty fair understanding of both styles of playing — Buckley's ("Guitar") and Butler's ("Banjo", or "Stroke") — I set about systematizing them in conformity with the rules and principles of music — an undertaking which was of inestimable value in pursuing the study of the instrument. Butler's playing, while effective, was far from artistic, and his *repertoire* limited chiefly to jigs, reels, walk-arounds and his comic songs.

He was of medium height, rather heavily built, of a genial disposition, played his solos sitting and in a "make-up" similar to that now worn by our comic solo players.

The next banjoist whom it was my good fortune to hear was "Hi" S. Rumsey, another "champion," who came along with "Garry" Hough's theatrical troupe. In those days the program usually comprised two plays; opening with tragedy or comedy and concluding with a light farce. Instead of an intermission between the plays it was the custom to introduce a specialty of some kind, generally a danseuse, but with this company Rumsey held that place.

No two banjoists ever contrasted more strongly in appearance, style, make-up and act than did Butler and Rumsey. Butler, short in stature, comparatively, in his patched, ill-fitting plantation get-up of old boots, exaggerated collar, slouch hat, etc.; suitable, however, for the character of his act, and sitting with one leg thrown across the other as he played and sang his plantation ditties; while Rumsey, an Apollo, standing fully six feet, of magnificent physique and straight as an arrow, was most fastidious in his dress. He played in his shirt sleeves, and standing, his banjo supported by a strap around his neck. His trousers were the flashiest of plaids or stripes, of faultless fit and strapped down over patent leather boots; an immaculately clean, fancy colored calico shirt, its heavily ruffled front standing out from a flower embroidered, single-breasted, low-cut vest, buttoned at the waist; a white felt hat with a red ribbon band, and with his banjo thrown carelessly over his shoulder he would jump on the stage with a characteristic laugh and a "Good ebenin', white folks," which was sure to gain the good will of his audience. His knowledge of the "Guitar" style was slight and limited to a few simple pieces and accompaniments. His stage work was with the thimble. He usually finished his solos with an exhibition of his abilities as a banjoist, playing such pieces as the Arkansas Traveler, Down on the Wabash, Grey Eagle, etc., displaying much skill in showy and brilliant execution. And in "trick work," imitating a hand organ by playing an air with his left hand while seemingly turning a crank with his right; or 'winding the clock," as he would tell his audience, by describing circles on the strings with his right hand running up and down the fingerboard while pulling them with his left, during which he would relate an amusing story of his grandfather's clock and the different ways he could wind it, which he would illustrate. He also gave an illustration of "Trinity Bell Chimes," by swinging the banjo with his left hand, and, aided by. the right held near it, executing the sounds of the bells. But proper that, some mention should be made of his principal rival, Tom Briggs, whom, however, I had heard but a few times. At that time the champion spirit was running high and there was no love lost between the two banjoists. Both had hosts of friends and admirers; but, of the two, Briggs, perhaps, was the most favorably esteemed; his pleasing voice and happy-go-lucky manner of playing tending to ingratiate him in the affections of his friends. Their respective superiority as players was a hotly disputed question, and, as they had never clashed in actual contest, will always so remain. In one respect, however, they bore close resemblance; both were gentlemanly, and ultra fashionable in their street attire. It was said of Briggs that he could be seen any pleasant day strolling on Broadway, the "best dressed man in town." He died in California, and it is related by Eph Horn, who attended him during his last illness, that his only comfort and solace was his banjo, which he kept constantly by his side on his bed. Shortly before his death and when he had become too weak to play, he placed his hand on his banjo and, looking at Eph, he said, with almost his expiring breath: "Hang it up, Eph, I'll never hit it again."

Banjo Reminiscences. III
Written Exclusively for 'THE CADENZA. August, 1901
BY FRANK B. CONVERSE, NEW YORK CITY.

Hipe Rumsey had another accomplishment—he was an expert with the drumsticks, and frequently varied his encores by introducing a drum solo. His "juggling of the sticks" while executing rolls and taps of every conceivable description, so rapidly that he seemed in a maze of flying, twirling sticks, his vivid, detonating punctuations, pianissimo and fortê effects were —so drummers said—"simply marvelous." His banjo enthusiasm he shared with his drum, a shallow, highly burnished nickel rim, which shone like a gem as he played. It was made for him by Wilson, of Troy, N. Y., who also was then making his banjos. Wilson's banjos, either nickel rim (which he created) or wood, were famous, and for symmetry in construction, brilliancy, and resonance have never been excelled. But of the banjo and its evolution later. [*ed. note: Wilson and his cohorts in Troy, N.Y. made the first generation of banjos with metal-clad rims – sometimes referred to as spun-over and later emulated by S.S. Stewart and other banjo-makers.*]

Sensitively conscious of his abilities, he, at times, was inclined to take himself too seriously, but on the whole was exceedingly gentlemanly and agreeable, and frequently visited my home, when he would play for me. [*ed.note: Rumsey was known as Hipe, Hi or Hy and was one of the earliest performers to give imitations of the bell chimes on the banjo and, unlike most of his contemporaries, Mr. Rumsey played while in a standing position.*]

In the height of his popularity he was stricken with paralysis of the spine, which terminated his professional career and eventually caused his death. During a long illness he was kindly remembered by his professional friends. At a benefit tendered to him in the Bowery, I had the pleasure of representing the banjo.

Quoting from a letter lately received from his brother Wm. W., also a banjoist and drummer of local fame, and residing in Newburgh, "Hipe was born June 12, 1828, was taken ill in 1864 and died Sept. 9, 1871. I gave his banjo to Andy Leavitt two or three years after his death. I didn't like it myself, it was too large. I can't give you the exact dimensions. It must have been about 13-inch head, about 4 inches deep, fingerboard at least 20 inches, wood rim. The brackets were of iron and very heavy, number about 30. He had two of the same dimensions and assembled them himself. The instrument was a load for anyone to carry, but oh! what a tone. I never heard anything like it. Hipe gave me my first banjo and one of your books, saying go away by yourself and learn yourself to play, as I did.

From Rumsey's departure to the time when I ventured upon my first engagement I can recollect of meeting but one more banjo player, and he a negro named Sam Pride— "Purnell," he sometimes said. He had a style of his own which was characteristic and included some attractive effects. He went to California, I believe, and may be there still.

My first engagement worth mentioning was with McFarland's Theatrical Company in 1855, then playing in Detroit, and where I succeeded Hi S. Rumsey, he having resigned. Remained with the company some time and terminated my engagement at London, C.W.

"Larry" Barrett—Lawrence, when later he had become the eminent tragedian—was a young member of the company; also Miss Maggie Mitchell when in Canada. Later I joined the Backus Minstrels (not "Charley" Backus of the San Francisco's),in Chicago, Ill., a newly organized company, which located at Odd Fellows' Hall, hoping to establish there ; a hope, however, which was not realized. "Mob" Turner, from New York, was with the company—stage manager. He could play the banjo fairly well and was, I understood, the originator of the miscalled "Simplified Method" which, I regret to say, is still in vogue with some teachers. Before leaving Chicago I again met "Pie" Butler, our first meeting since the Elmira episode, and had the satisfaction of convincing him of the advantages to be derived from a knowledge of the principles of music.

Learning that the banjo was a very popular instrument in St. Louis, I went there and engaged in teaching. The spirit of banjo rivalry had preceded me and I was not overlooked by the western "champions;" but as details of old banjo contests would be of no special interest to the readers of The Cadenza, I refrain from their mention, excepting one, however, for which, as it involved my prestige as a competent teacher, and created considerable comment, I crave the reader's indulgence.

My presumptive challenger, presumptive from long popularity, especially among the river men, who urged the question was a Western "champion" by the name of Kelley. At that time Prendergast ("Tom"), Newcomb ("Bill') and Bryant's ("Dan") Minstrels were at Wyman's Hall, and the contest, which they billed, took place during one of their performances, they furnishing the prize—a pair of solid gold miniature deer horns. In those days of steamboat racing on the Mississippi River it was the custom for the fastest and best passenger boat to adorn its "Texas" (pilot house) with a large pair of deer's antlers, hence the significance of the prize.

The event drew a crowded house. We didn't play for "points"—whatever that may mean. There were no particular details governing the match—a sort of go- as-you-please affair, the decision being left to the audience, who kindly awarded me the horns.

Parenthetically, I would add that this was the usual result of my various experiences, and simply demonstrates the supremacy of musical principles vs. simplified, ear or other methods.

This occurred in the latter part of 1856, and before Bryant's Minstrels were organized and established at Mechanic's Hall, 472 Broadway, New York, by the brothers Jerry, Dan and Neil. New York never had more popular performers or greater favorites. Dan and Jerry "had the ends" respectively with tambourine and bones, and Neil's artistic Flutina solo was an attractive feature. Prominent among the "fixtures" of the company were "Tom" Prendergast, the sweet voiced tenor, whose delightful rendering of "Sally in Our Alley" will never be forgotten by those who were favored to hear him—it seemed *his* Sally of whom he sang.

Nelse Seymour, comedian and nearly a good banjoist; rollicking Nelse, brimming over with good humor—I don't believe he had an enemy in the world. "Sher" Campbell, the superb baritone, statuesque, polished, exquisite—you'd mistake him for a society swell. George Weeks, tenor robusto, who also sang in a fashionable church choir, from which he was dismissed when it was discovered that he was a minstrel! He became hopelessly insane a few years ago and died recently at an asylum in Middletown, N. Y. Ned Winchell, now a resident of Chicago and engaged in business, was for a long time connected with Bryant's; a fine musician, excellent banjoist and composer. There were others but I'll mention only one more.

"Jim" Unsworth, the banjoist. He came from Canada and introduced a brogue in his banjo songs that made a hit. He was a most promising banjo student, but became a better comedian, to which line he later gave his attention. After Bryant's he 'doubled" with "Eugene," female impersonator, and with him located with a company in Liverpool, England, as banjoist and comedian, where he died.

Dick Parker, an excellent and, at one time, popular banjoist, was previously with this company, eventually returning to the United States. Dan Bryant's forte was *not* banjo. However, he could play "a little," enough, with his comicalities to help him through his funny solos. He once engaged to take lessons, but after receiving a few concluded that Providence never designed him to be a banjoist. And this reminds me that throughout my experience I have rarely met a black-face comedian—a really funny man—who was also a fine banjo player. However, I can recall a few exceptions, notably E. M. Hall, whom I first met in a professional way many years ago in Chicago where I was teaching in connection with "Charley" Harris, an old- time banjoist whom I once chanced to excel in a friendly "seance" in his native town, Goshen, Indiana. Of E. M. Hall it has been well said that he "has kept pace with the advance and development of the instrument and is thus qualified to personally illustrate any phase of banjo playing up to date."

And Sam Devere. I remember him way back in '65, doing banjo solos at Harry Enoch's in Philadelphia. An "up-to-date" banjoist was lost to the world when Sam decided to rest on the laurels he so early gathered, and adopt the comic role. Judging from results, doubtless he has been wise in his generation.

And of Billy Carter about the same may be said. Billy was a young man in New Orleans the winter (1857) I played there at "Dave" Bidwell's Theatre with Matt Peel's Campbell Minstrels, having joined this company in St. Louis, Mo., and again succeeding Rumsey who, with "Bill" Newcomb, thereupon organized a minstrel company and preceded us down the Mississippi at all towns where we were billed and played same season in New Orleans.

Billy has since told me that hearing me play gave him the impulse to learn the instrument. Later—more than twenty years and he had long been a professional player, he became a most promising pupil at my "studio" (called instruction rooms then) at 555 Broadway, but, like his contemporary Sam Devere, he, etc., etc. I remember his expression when speaking of the great advantage a knowledge of music, which he had then acquired, afforded him. He said it was "like letting down the bars and turning him loose into a twenty acre lot." A unique, but rather comprehensive comparison. J. K. Camell, another old- timer, also had fine ideas, but chose to rest on the comic solo stratum. He was a favorite at R. M. (Dick) Hooley's Minstrels in Brooklyn and Chicago as far back as 1871.

Did space permit, many others might be recalled, worthy of special mention, whose proficiency in playing has contributed to popularize the instrument. But it has never lacked students,—painstaking, conscientious workers, champions —yes, champions! For, irrespective of modern criticism, much can be said for them. Admitting that the day of "musical sparring bouts," the "pugilistic banjo age," etc., is passed, it was but the natural outcome of conditions, and it is to those contentious, ambitious enthusiasts, animated by a spirit of jealousy and emulation, that the present development of the instrument is largely due. And while deprecating a restoration, I seriously question if the same spirit does not still slumber in the emotions of the present generation.

[ed. note: In Lowell Schreyer's The Banjo Entertainers (Mankato,MN: Minnesota Heritage Pub 2007) the partisanship of critics and fans as regards banjo contests recounts careers established and ruined by acclaim and disrepute – especially in the case of Frank Converse. Show business tabloids such as the New York Clipper wrote at length about the minstrel companies and individual performers and noted the results of contests and formal competitions]

Banjo Reminiscences. IV

Written Exclusively for THE CADENZA. September, 1901
BY FRANK B. CONVERSE, NEW YORK CITY.

Of the pioneers who fostered the banjo in its infant days the first to be mentioned is Joel Walker Sweeney, who gave us the instrument, and, it is said, was the "Father of Minstrelsy." This latter claim, however, seems in doubt, as it is said that T. D. Rice— "Daddy Rice," the original "Jump Jim Crow"—was the first to black his face. Again, the question is raised in favor of Jim Sanford, a banjoist of the period, who was traveling and playing solos in 1833. It is said of Joe Sweeney that he not only blacked his face, but his neck, arms and feet as well and came on the stage in his bare feet carrying a sawbuck, on which he sat, though he often played standing.

"Old Dan" Emmet was contemporary with Sweeney, but best known throughout the North. He played at the old Chatham Theatre. He was doubtless the best banjoist of the time—his knowledge of music aiding him—and composer of the best banjo songs. He also played the violin and was famous for his jig playing. Upon the organization of Bryant's Minstrels he joined them and composed most of the "Walk-arounds" for that company, including the still popular "Way Down South in Dixie." This venerable pioneer of the banjo is still living in Mt. Vernon, Ohio, a beneficiary of the Actors' Fund.

Pete Jenkins was a very popular player in 1839 and displayed a refined Phase in his playing, accompanying his voice with his banjo and singing "The Ivy Green' and other descriptive songs.

A very eccentric "ancient," the mention of whose name provoked a smile, was Dave ("Dad") Lull. History fails to record his first appearance as a banjoist, or on earth, but he was one of the earliest, even before minstrel troupes were organized. In 1842 he had long been a favorite at the old Eagle Street Theatre in Buffalo. He was a humpback of the most pronounced type. He was a jig dancer and played "Juba" for his own dancing, which was grotesque.

Frank Stanton, a studious, painstaking banjoist, was playing at Charley White's Melodeon in the Bowery in 1846.

Julius A. Von Bonhurst was considered an artistic player with Sam S. Sanford's Minstrels in 1851.

Bill Ray, a deservedly popular banjoist and versatile performer from 1850 to '66, was lost at sea on the *Evening Star* in the latter year.

Earl Pierce, a favorite comic solo player, who sang "Hoop-de-dooden-doo," was long with E. P. Christy's Minstrels, 472 Broadway. He went to England with Raynor's Christy's and was succeeded by Tom Vaughn, who was accounted a good jig player. Illness eventually compelled Vaughn's retirement from the stage, and he was removed to the City Hospital on Blackwell's Island, where he died.

And there was Andy Leavitt, who also wrote negro sketches, and Jim Clarke, who made and introduced shallow rim, thin-toned, nickel banjos, and Luke West and Matt Peel, comedians, who traveled together; G. W. ("Pony") Moore, proprietor of Christy's Minstrels, London, England, and the Morris brothers—Lou, Bill and Charley—whose minstrel company was located in Boston, where they were great favorites; and Sam Sharpley, Ben Cotton, Bill Newcomb, Billy Arlington, Billy Sweatman, Billy Whitlock, Tom Chatfield.

Pupsey Keenan, who was with Henry Wood and George Christy's Minstrels at 444 Broadway in 1854, singing "On de oder side of Hobuck" in Dutch, and of whom it is related that - like Tom Briggs—when on his deathbed he called for his banjo and endeavored to play, but only produced a faint sound. Smiling sadly, he drew the instrument to his breast and peacefully passed away.

And Jim Johnson, a Western champion; Bill Lehr, another, and Charley Morrell, who also made banjos; Bill Donaldson, who in 1850 used to astonish the people with his left-hand playing —occasionally reversing his banjo; and Jake Wallace and George Coes, the California champion, with whom I once "tilted" satisfactorily in San Francisco—all prominent old-timers, and, with barely few exceptions, "thimble" players. Charley Morrell was a maker of fine banjos in New York in the early fifties, and organized the "first banjo tournament in America," which took place at the Chinese Assembly Rooms, No. 539 Broadway, New York, Oct. 19, 1857.

The following are the main particulars of the tournament, extracted from a letter written by Mr. Morrell in 1890, a short time before his decease. The prize was a $100 banjo.

There were twenty contestants, among whom the following were the most prominent: Picayune Butler, Phil Rice, Chas. Plummer, Frank Speed, C. Hunter, T. Harris, Ed Chappel, Andy Roome and M. Tierney. The judges had no particular understanding as to "points," and based their decision on "general principles" and were greatly influenced by the applause given the respective players.

"At 8 o'clock there were three thousand people in the hall and a great many on the outside, trying to get in. The hall was so packed that many ladies in the audience fainted and had to be taken out the rear entrance, as it was impossible to get out the front door."

The three judges awarded the prize to Charles Plummer, a banjoist from Brooklyn, also the title of "Champion Banjoist," much to the dissatisfaction of Picayune Butler's friends.

At that time I was traveling through the Southern States with Matt Peel's Campbell Minstrels, and, also dissatisfied with the decision, challenged the winner, including all the contestants, in the columns of the *New York Clipper*—the first public challenge of which there is any record. The challenge was issued at the suggestion of "Pony" Moore (above mentioned), then a member of our company (tambourinist and comedian), who was willing to risk $500 on the result—as stated in the challenge. Soon after, our company located in New York. For some reason or other the challenge went unnoticed.

What an interesting volume the multitudinous incidents occurring in the lives of our banjoists would make! And this recalls a bit of experience with an amusing side that befell me early in 1857 with a small company got together to play some of the small towns in Southern Illinois. "Egypt," they had named that portion of the State, and rightly, too, I concluded, after my experience. We were billed to appear in a small village—a mere hamlet in fact, situated not many miles north of Cairo on the Mississippi river, the town of which it was said they'd never take the census unless several steamboats with big passenger lists were at the levee. Our train having been delayed, we had no time to spare to reach the hall and dress. As it was, we were a little late in getting ready, but what surprised us was the silence reigning "in front." Usually an audience kept waiting after the hour is inclined to give pronounced manifestation of its impatience. But not a sound reached us. Considerate, we thought; nice people, etc., etc. Finally, all being ready and each man standing at his chair, I couldn't resist drawing the curtain aside and taking a preliminary look at so seemingly model an assemblage.

Yes—there they were—the benches! But empty ! — or nearly so—not more than a dozen people "holding them down," and not a woman among them!

But how did it happen?

Surely our clear-headed agent was three days ahead—must have billed the town, and no opposition that we knew of. Simply inexplicable.

However, we went on and gave the show, though it seemed like playing for a funeral—all the applause coming from the echoes we stirred up. But the mystery which lasted overnight was cleared up on the following morning. Yes, our agent had attended to his business; our one-sheet posters were still to be seen on sheds, barns, fences and big trees; but adjoining each was tacked another—a *written* "poster"—a foolscap sheet filled with selections from the book of Proverbs running as follows: "My son, if sinners entice thee, consent thou not." "Even in laughter the heart is made sorrowful." I only remember these, but the others were like unto them. Later we learned from the sexton that, as a further precaution to meet the emergency, an extra experience meeting was called for that evening, and *there was our audience!*

The pastor had watched his flock; the admonishing proverbs had "got in their work;" and our show?—it was killed!

But the sexton—who exercised the functions of undertaker as well—was a pretty decent person who, besides some excellent advice, gave me a good recipe for perspiring hands—from which I was not free—that made some amends for our loss. It may interest some of your readers to know what it is.

Dissolve alum in a half-tumbler of water - as much as the water will take up; add an equal quantity of alcohol and the prescription is filled. Before playing, bathe the hands or finger-tips for several minutes.

Returning to our topic : It is interesting to note that throughout the history of the banjo and its world of players, the instances are rare where a negro has attained sufficient prominence as a player to attract special notice. Even when this has happened it has been due to his sensational, grotesque or gymnastic manipulation rather than any display of either true musical merit or artistic excellence.

This statement is in no sense to be construed as disparaging to the colored man, as such, or respecting his musical faculty, which is admittedly congenital with his race; but merely as stating a fact, account for it as we may. However, it is a fact of much significance as confirming what was asserted in a former article respecting the banjo, its origin and progress, and the character of those who have developed its capabilities.

Conceding that there have been some remarkably sensational colored players, it will doubtless be contended by some that the assertion asserts too much, that instances have been sufficiently numerous to question it. But it might be replied that the world has witnessed marvelous phenomena in the mental field; that psychological eccentricities are not infrequent; that we are familiar with lightning calculators, mind-readers, prodigies, beings endowed with extraordinary mental or physical powers; musical phenomenons—Blind Tom, for instance, a piano phenomenon, and without much mental process; and "things being as they are," it seems not an unreasonable supposition that many of the instances which could be cited might be referred to these phenomena.

Of all the colored players who have been much in evidence, it is generally conceded that the name of Horace Weston bears undisputed pre-eminence. Unquestionably, Weston was a musical genius, as attested by his ability to play on a variety of instruments, to some extent. His biographer has said that he first essayed the accordion, which he mastered when but seven years of age; at ten he could play the violin, and then followed the violoncello, double bass, slide trombone and guitar. He was also an expert dancer. But that he was an artist – opinions differ.

Genius alone does not constitute the artist. That's the foundation. But something more is essential—a mental *something* that observes much, 'thinks much to— so to speak—complete the superstructure.

That Weston was a remarkable and highly sensational executant *in his way*, will not be disputed, or that he could produce many novel and startling effects; but they were distinctly his own—they were "Weston" and ceased with him.

Although familiar with many instruments, he excelled with the banjo, and it is as a banjoist that the world knew him; for he had traveled extensively here and abroad—a sensation in London, Berlin, Breslau, Vienna, Hamburg, through France; and in this country with various companies, at watering-places, on steamboats, in saloons, beer gardens, etc., from about the age of 30 nearly up to the time of his death in 1890.

When playing, he preferred to be seated in an arm chair, with the rim of his banjo resting upon one of the arms, which gave a solid support for the instrument, and so increased its tone volume.

His favorite banjo was of full size, with a shallow rim. He preferred light strings. His bridge, very narrow and low—much narrower than the ordinary violin bridge— he placed quite near to the tail-piece in order to obtain a nasal quality of tone, which he fancied. The narrow bridge also enabled him to execute a very novel, if not very musical, effect which he produced by rubbing the tip of his extended thumb rapidly to and fro across the strings, causing a buzzing sound which he would introduce *ad libitum* for various purposes.

It can be truthfully said of Weston that, as an exemplar of certain possibilities—musical or otherwise—of which the instrument seems susceptible—he was unrivaled. [*ed. note: While ravelling in Europe with the Jarrett and Palmer organization, Weston was summoned for a command performance before Queen Victoria. Some months earlier he won a banjo contest in New York City's Steinway Hall, beating Charles and Edward Dobson, among others].*

Sam Pride, a colored player whom I have mentioned, was a neat and quite artistic player with the thimble, and introduced some fine effects. He could execute a trill with such rapidity that, when upon strings stopped in unison, it approximated a sustained tone.

A perfect trill in the guitar style of fingering seems quite impracticable. It is certainly too fine an effect to be omitted by the finished player, and can easily be acquired by observing, for the time, Sam Pride's style of execution.

The Bohee brothers, James and George, colored, were noted "thimble" players of the Weston "school," though not so robust and demonstrative in their execution, in fact aspiring to the refined. Gentlemanly and unassuming in demeanor, they were doubly popular with the public. They frequently traveled in company with Weston, and were prominent factors of the combination. They went to London, England, several years ago where, meeting with public favor as players and teachers, they remained.

Blackman (or Blankman), an old-time colored player, of Troy, N. Y., is credited with having applied the tremolo movement to the banjo over thirty years ago. That was before the advent in this country of the mandolin.

Query: Had Blackman heard the mandolin and so conceived the idea of substituting the forefinger for the plectrum? For that's its action—the addition being the accompaniment with the thumb.

However that may be, what a field of opportunities the "tremolo" opened for the banjoist! Its beautiful effect was quickly recognized and the movement appropriated by the players of the day— Harry Stanwood, Lew Brimmer, and others, who were not slow in popularizing and disseminating it with their "Home, Sweet Home," while playing an accompaniment with the thumb.

I specially mention Stanwood and Brimmer, as they were among the first to "spread" the tremolo, and at that time were New York favorites— Stanwood with Billy Emerson's California Minstrels at 720 Broadway, and Brimmer with Henry Wood's Minstrels, Broadway, opposite the old St. Nicholas Hotel. I mention Stanwood first as he was the better banjoist.

A knowledge of music — which Brimmer lacked — enabled him to study the instrument intelligently, and of the two (they both attended at my studio) he was the most studious and ambitious. Harry Stanwood was a Canadian. He had received a liberal education, was well versed in music, had a fine conception of the banjo, and had he lived would have attained high rank as an artist.

Although affecting the comic role, he was not an Ethiopian comedian, and his solos and incidental "remarks" were comparatively of a refined character.

Lew Brimmer, on the contrary, was drollery personified, either on or off the stage, very original in his "remarks," and the originator of many of the slang phrases that "went the rounds." He was a "happy-go-lucky," and lived in the present. But for this he might have become a fine banjoist. He boasted much of his "educated finger," as he expressed it, referring to the tremolo movement, in the execution of which he assumed he could not be approached, and would say that "when he dropped it on 'old Culinary' (a heavy metal rim banjo presented to him by an enterprising maker, for business reasons, and which he occasionally introduced) it made the angels weep."

A good, all-around player, he was also, unfortunately, a "good fellow," and to the frailties of too good fellowship and its associations may be attributed the untimely closing of a promising career and his early taking off, with "none so poor to do him reverence."

Poor Lew!—his own worst enemy—led a chequered life, and his misfortunes were "thick upon him," but his drollery often served him a good turn.

Many a good story is told of him and his ready adaptability in exigencies.

He once was traveling out West with a company which stranded at a small town on the Mississippi river. By some stratagem the company succeeded in decamping, leaving Lew on the levee with only his banjo, among strangers, and not a nickel in his exchequer. Sitting on a bale of cotton and deploring his ill-luck, he was aroused from his musing by the arrival of a steamboat.

His hopes brightened. Possibly he might be able to beg passage, indifferent as to its termination. Throwing his banjo over his shoulder and venturing on board, he sauntered around, hoping to attract attention, but nothing came of it.

Finally, when about to cast off the lines and it became *then or never* for Lew, he sought the Captain, only to be gruffly ordered ashore—and "mighty quick, too."

Lew eyed him for a moment, as if sounding him, walked deliberately ashore, unlimbered his banjo and, standing at the water's edge, commenced singing "We Parted by the River's Side," in a voice so loud that it attracted the attention of all on board. The Captain stood amazed at the audacious coolness of the proceeding, but he proved not devoid of humor, and quickly grasping the "pat" but ludicrous application of the song, burst into a hearty laugh and with an expression more assuring than polite told Lew to "git on,' and throughout the passage and until New Orleans was reached only "the best was good enough for Lew."

This obituary was published shortly after Lew's death.

"The Dead Minstrel" (from *The New York Sun*)

'I knew Louis Brimmer very well' said Billy Birch yesterday, speaking of the minstrel who died in jail at Canajoharie on Saturday. 'He was a fine banjo player and a good singer years ago, and we enjoyed him while we were at 586 Broadway, but his habits made it impossible to depend on him. He had talent and might have been a good deal of a man if he had improved his chances'.

'Lew Brimmer's last appearance in New York,' said Sandy Spencer, 'was in my music hall in the

Bowery in June last.' He was born in Cooperstown forty-two years ago and came to New York in 1861. Among people who heard him when he was a banjo soloist at Henry Wood's Minstrels at 514 Broadway, there is but one opinion. He was the best banjo player in the country. He could draw wonderful music from the banjo up to the last. But, if you hired him on Saturday for a Monday evening engagement in New York, he was as likely to be in Pittsburg on Monday as here.

'I remember,' said an actor, 'that when Lew Brimmer was with the San Franciscos, Backus was summoned to Rochester by the sudden illness of a relative, and Bernard said: Mr. Brimmer, I want you to play the end.'

"I came here to plunkett" (pick the banjo), Lew answered. "Well," Bernard says, "this is a case of must. And you have got to play the end."

"He rehearsed in splendid shape but at 7:30 in the evening he had not appeared. Bernard went all over for him. At 7:50 he came stumbling in, peculiarly jolly. There was no time for a change and they knew he had good nerve, as he went on with the rest but he was too hilarious for the stock jokes, and besides that, he was in Backus's clothes which would go twice around him, and was the most ludicrous subject you can imagine.

"Now the trouble begins," he said, as they took their seats and that brought the house down. The San Franciscos have that phrase yet at the top of their bills.

"How do you feel, Mr. Brimmer?" Wambold said.

"I feel like a hired man." Brimmer replied, and his comical appearance, and the absence of Backus made the remark so apropos that the house went wild.

"But his stay with the San Franciscos was short. One night he went out to sing "Old Zip Coon" in a frightful condition. Wambold tried to call him off the stage but he wouldn't come. The they rang the curtain down. Before he went home that night they handed him his envelope with a notion of his discharge. He looked at it and tore it up.

"On Monday he was on hand for rehearsal as usual. Birch looked at Wambold and Wambold looked at Backus. "Hasen't he got his notice? Wambold said. Of course he has," Backus replied; I saw Billy writing it."

"Well, give him another week, and then we'll serve the notice on him." When the second notice was served he tore it up and came in on Monday as before. The partners called him in again and told him he must know he was discharged.

"Do you mean this? he said.

"Yes sir."

"Well, a jokes a joke," he said. "But if you do that again, I'll quit."

"I got acquainted with him and with his ugly stub-tailed dog in California," said a variety actor. "The dog used to go with the boys when they went out for a time, and took his glass of beer with the rest. When the dog was intoxicated he would go off and hide himself until he was sober."

"I was with him in Massachusetts," said another, "traveling with a provincial company, when he made that joke on a young English actor. There were not many dressing rooms and the young Englishman was dressing behind the wood front with which the stage was set. Just as the fellow was in the midst of his toilet, standing with his back to the audience, Brimmer blew the whistle and the sides were run back. The audience cheered tremendously, but the sides were hurried together again. The Englishman never looked around or noticed anything."

"Excuse me," he said to Brimmer, a moment afterward, "but that fellow who was just on made a bloody good hit."

"John Toppin, treasurer of Harry Miner's new theater," said another, "had a characteristic experience two or three years ago with Brimmer. He found him on a tramp in Connecticut, took him to a hotel, renovated him, and brought him to New York. Toppin hired a theater for a benefit for Lew, and finally sold the whole house. On the day of the performance, Brimmer began drinking and when evening came he was in an awful condition. As he saw the crowds pressing into the theater he said to an acquaintance, "I hope they'll have a good time." An hour later he took a train for the west.

It was two years afterward that Toppin found him in wretched plight warming himself behind a stove in Sandy Spencer's "Live and Let Live and fixed him up again."

Banjo Reminiscences. V
Written Exclusively for THE CADENZA. October 1901
BY FRANK B. CONVERSE, NEW YORK CITY.

To the widely spread publicity born of the Morrell Banjo Tournament may be largely attributed the engendering of the spirit of rivalry—I might say banjo belligerency—which raged with increasing asperity up to 1867, the year of the Dobson - Buckley controversy.

To be chronologically correct, it should be incidentally mentioned that some time previous to this fiasco—for so it proved— the banjo-playing members of the Dobson family, then not very extensively known, and whose acquaintance the writer had not formed—exhibited a restless desire for a banjo record and, having singled out the writer as a promising opportunity, proceeded with most assiduous persistency to publicly contrast proficiencies, much to the disparagement of the writer and further, occasionally approaching the verge of personal collision, as if such a course might help to emphasize the possession of superior banjo qualifications—on general principles.

Finally, indifference yielding to persistency of attack and desirous of disposing of the subject effectually, a challenge was published in the *New York Clipper* which----- that there might be no charge of slighting--included all the banjo-aspiring members of the family.

If I recall it correctly, the wager was $500.

As anticipated by the writer, nothing resulted but a protracted and somewhat acrimonious weekly controversy in the columns of the *Clipper*, week and week about. The ostensible cause of the failure was the writer's insistence that the judges should be musicians, which was opposed by the challenged party as an entirely superfluous qualification. And so the effort was dropped. However, that no doubtful inference should remain, the writer decided to prepare a contestant who might prove more acceptable, and here is where Mr. J. K. Buckley enters.

At this time Mr. Buckley could play well, and it was an open question respecting the relative banjoic merits of himself and the Dobsons, and as this relationship was in a state of agitation Mr. Buckley was not averse to a contest; so, after two or three months of preparation with the writer, he challenged the family through the *Clipper*, for $1,500, Mr. A. R. ("Sandy") Spencer (a friend of the writer) depositing certified check for that amount.

Sandy was the proprietor of a café adjoining Henry Woods' Minstrel Hall on Broadway. His place was a rendezvous for minstrels and other professionals. He was a fair banjoist himself, and always kept a fine banjo or two for the convenience of his banjo playing patrons. It was here that the meetings (and wranglings) were held and where the writer, in the interests of Mr. Buckley, endeavored to adjust differences, but ineffectually, as the same principal objection was again interposed; and after a renewal of newspaper hostilities in the *Clipper*, this second attempt to bring about an issue received its quietus in a vigorous editorial by Frank Queen (deceased), then editor and proprietor of the *Clipper*, which, censuring the tactics of the party of the first part, was highly complimentary of Mr. Buckley. Mr. Buckley still lives, and his fingers seem not to have lost their cunning. [*ed.note: Buckley (born in New York City in 1839) was a highly regarded banjo player and started Buckley's Minstrels in Newark, NJ in 1868.*]

Of all the banjo contests that have occurred within the range of the writer's experience, there was but one instance wherein the color line was not drawn and, oddly enough, this was in the vicinity of the fighting ground of the "Border War."

In 1884, when Kansas City, Mo., was enjoying its boom days, there came from Pittsburgh, Pa., a colored man, an "ear player," Stinson by name, whose banjo playing attracted more than ordinary notice. His pieces were mostly new to that locality, and as he could play them well he was soon in high favor, and there developed in his head the self-congratulating notion that he was just "monarch of all he surveyed," — a conclusion he exhibited no particular delicacy in proclaiming. But there were others - white players, with pre-empted claims, who objected to this usurpation, were little disposed to take kindly to the presumptive assumptiveness of the 'dark horse.' So felt Dan Polk: so felt others; but it is of Dan Polk I write—a really fine executant, who enjoys the further distinction of having been the first to introduce the mandolin pick on the banjo. His friends, confident of his superior abilities and determined that they should be acknowledged, decided there should be a contest. Interest on the probabilities ran high, for the colored man had gained many admirers of his playing. The rest can be easily and briefly told. The event came off at the Ninth Street Museum during the regular vaudeville Performance and the decision was left to the audience, which by general acclamation pronounced in favor of Polk-—so scoring another victory for correct principles and the banjoists of Kansas City were appeased.

In calling the roll of the early banjoists I would be remiss indeed were I to overlook Mr. Fred Mather, a gentleman residing in Brooklyn, N.Y., whose many accomplishments and experiences, if written, would fill a book. As a showman he was, as expressed in stage vernacular, a 'general utility'' and exceptionally an understudy "all over the bill"; a fine banjo soloist, excellent straight jig dancer, female impersonator ("wench dancer" in those days), *au fait* on either end—with bones or tambourine—and I believe it no exaggeration to say he could have done a ballad in an emergency. And more. As a patriotic citizen he "washed up" and went to the front in our war of the rebellion, serving with distinction on the field of glory. Though all fields seemed alike to him, the literary field next presented the most alluring attractions, and as a writer his graceful pen, wielded in many contributions to the press and otherwise, has earned him a most enviable prominence—a realization of the truism that the pen is mightier than the sword, in proof of which I have only to mention his contributions to *Forest and Stream* entitled 'Men I Have Fished With," which have since been published in book form.

I am indebted to Mr. J. E. Henning, of Chicago, a gentleman of well established prominence in the musical world as writer, composer, teacher, inventor and manufacturer of superlatively fine banjos, for permission to extract the following from a letter of Mr. Mather's received by him some time since.

Mr. Mather writes as follows: "I knew Old Joe' Sweeney about or between 1846 and 1848, when I was a boy of thirteen to fifteen. He came North with a circus twice in different years. He taught me how to bring down my thumb and play the Grape Vine Twist.' Old Joe ! I have often wondered 'why old?' As near as I can remember he was not over thirty then - Perhaps his song:

Old Joe a kickin' up behind and befo',

An' a yaller gal kickin' up behind old Joe'

was the origin . I believe there is no doubt that he was the first to put the thumb string on the banjo, the 'chaunter' or chanter we called it then, but I have not heard that word in years."

Old Dan Emmet was the great banjo man of the day. His forte was in stringing off nonsense and making it sound well. He played jigs for me in very slow time, 'Old Folks at Home' as slow as Parepa Rosa sang it: my doubles and trebles on the sanded floor put in all the variations.

'Old Dan used to sing Talk all de night long, de night long.

What's dat down dar dat you pick up?

Shoo shall de Egyptian

Walk tro de garden to Jerusalem.

Rock. Susanna, do fare you well, etc.

Old Simon Buckhart, de hearty, hearty hart

He kep' a full sale grocery store, an'

Had two peck measures; one held two quarts

and de odder didn't hold half a pint;

No : not by a jug. full.

And such stuff that wouldn't go now, but was original then, and took."

When traveling with Murphy, West and Peel's Minstrels back in the fifties (both Luke West and Matt Peel were comic banjo soloists as well as comedians) Mr. Mather continues:

"The hailing sign of the Know Nothings of those days was to take a pin from the left hand lapel of the coat.

Once when I went on in place of Luke West (who was indisposed) in Albany, I laid the banjo down, gazed at the stage, picked up a pin, straightened it with my teeth and put it on my coat and the house went wild. Luke took the thing up later and made a hit.

"When I did the 'Cocoanut Dance' with Matt Peel we did not mind an encore. I think that dance has never been revived. We had the shells on each knee, one on the breast and one on each hand, and we made up as South Sea Islanders."

Further on he writes: "I am not in it now although I keep an old time banjo, vintage of 1860, in a corner of my den and plunk on it in an old time way, never taking kindly to six strings or frets, especially the latter. I have forgotten most that I could play and learn nothing new, and fully realize that the banjo world has moved since I began plunking, over half a century ago." [ed. note: *Mather was also a banjo maker and an example of his work survives in the Smithsonian Institution. His wife presented the instrument to the museum in 1900. In one of his fishing treatises Mather recalled the banjo of old: "There were banjos in those days. They are rare now. They have put frets on them and made them merely guitars with a calf-skin head, on which can be played operatic music, but not real banjo music, which in these degenerate days is called "rag time." Just as negro minstrelsy has decayed, because of the abandonment of the "plantation" darky, so has our national instrument been evolved into a nondescript thing which has lost its individuality. Possibly this is because the abolition of slavery has divested the negro of a certain interest as a character to be sketched."]*

Mentioning Matt Peel reminds me of a little banjo act I originated when traveling with his company (mentioned in a former article), and which I did with him. We called it "The Siamese Twins," made up as Siamese, and were secured together by an elastic strap. Sitting close together and one passing his arm around the other, enabled each to hold and stop the strings upon the other's banjo while employing his right hand upon his own. Of course we played the same pieces and precisely alike, and so it was nothing more than each playing his own banjo; but it didn't so appear to the audience; it was mystifying, and deemed a remarkable feat. The act, which was introduced by our lecturer with a few appropriate remarks describing Nature's wonderful freak, was varied with songs and conversation a la Siamese, and made particularly amusing by quarrels in which each tried to withdraw in opposite directions, and the troubles which followed.

As with Mr. Mather's "Cocoanut Dance," I think the act has never been revived.

Another early one—E.H. (Ned) Winchell, whom I briefly noticed in a former article, may well lay claim to being an old time banjoist and as one who has contributed much to advance the instrument. Our acquaintance was formed in the early fifties and at one time we were in the same company – Matt Peel's Campbells. I know of no minstrel performer whose experience has had a broader range, in and out of the show business, and verily what he could relate would furnish a most interesting volume to Fred Mather's "book".

Versatile he too was a general understudy in any emergency and "at home with the banjo (at one time heralded as the 'Lion Banjoist'), bones, tambourine, violin, brass, jig or Interlocutor, as occasion might demand, and when tired of the stage, a broker, jeweler, promoter, speculator; at one time ringmaster with Spaulding & Rogers' circus, at another, on the

Mississippi river in 1860, managing a side show on the steamboat "James Raymond," which towed a smaller boat named 'The Floating Palace," that had been converted into a floating Amusement Hall for giving entertainments at the different landings and along the bayous not navigable for boats of usual draught. It was a boast of the captain that "The Palace could run on a heavy dew."

I take pleasure in acknowledging my indebtedness to him for much that follows.

In 1839 he heard Pete Jenkins (of whom I have written) sing the "Ivy Green," accompanying himself with his banjo and, as he expressed it, he was "dead gone on the instrument."

To quote him further : "The next day I bargained to have one made and got it in about a week. It was a beauty. Pine neck, pine pegs, a peck measure rim, a white sheepskin head tacked on. and I went at it for keeps. My mother allowed mc to take it to bed with me every night and I plunked myself to sleep, as happy as a child could be." In 1847 he had his first experience with a minstrel show, of which he says "It was called Evans' Minstrels and, considering the times, they were good. Some of its members were Jack Huntley, Frank Moran, Bill Elliott, Juba (colored), the best dancer that ever lived, and Gus Mead, the best banjo player I ever heard until I saw and heard you. He could beat Briggs, Rumsey, Pic Butler or any of them as long as he lived," Later, in '47, he went to Boston, uniting with Bill Newcomb, and Bige Thayer (both banjoists and comedians who had a statuary and minstrel show – odd combination!

Speaking of them:

"Newcomb was always good as a comedian and banjoist, and great in his burlesque lecture, but Thayer was *the* banjo-player and could play as well as either Briggs or Rumsey ever could."

For want of space I must, for the present, forego further mention of incidents relating to Mr. Winchell but must say that throughout his long professional career he was a prominent representative of the banjo, and his experience includes association with nearly every first- class company which flourished during the palmy days of minstrelsy.

Changing the subject, I wonder how many know that P. Gilmore, leader of Gilmore's famous brass band, may have got his inspiration from playing a tambourine in a minstrel band? No, not that exactly, for he was a very poor player but I'll let Winchell tell it. "When I went to Boston in 1849, Pat Gilmore was then playing the tambourine with Ordway's Aeolian Minstrels. Jerry Bryant was playing the bones. I met him on the street, when he told me that Pat Gilmore, the afterwards great leader of Gilmore's Band, couldn't play the tambourine *any*, and that there was an opening for me. We went to the hall where I played for Ordway, was engaged at once, went on that night and *Pat* was off the bill." Strange!

Banjo Reminiscences. VI

Written Exclusively for THE CADENZA. November 1901
BY FRANK B. CONVERSE, NEW YORK CITY.

Still with the old-timers! Truly a subject which might furnish most interesting material for many good-sized volumes. But it is not the present purpose to enter largely into history or incorporate within the limit allotted me irrelevant details of the lives of our banjo veterans, believing that the main object will be best subserved and the sketches made more interesting if limited to pertinent mentions of the early-day players and their personalities, including those principally who may be said to have helped to shape the destiny of the banjo, with such little incidents and anecdotes within my recollection, or I may have been able to glean from the past, and with which their names may be associated.

Contemporary with Briggs, Rumsey, Butler, Winchell and Arlington was Ben Cotton.

Born in Pawtucket, R. I., July 27, 1829, he still lives, despite the vicissitudes of a long and eventful professional service covering half a century; and a better preserved, sprightlier, happier or more active septuagenarian would be difficult to find. Although now extensively engaged in the laundry business up in 124th Street, Hancock Place, his old stage ardor remains undiminished, and, to paraphrase, scratch the laundryman and you'll find a minstrel; for nothing pleases him better than chatting with his friends over the incidents of his professional life during those happy old minstrel days. and his mind teems with reminiscences.

In evidence of his early predilection for the stage, he relates the following anecdote: He was but a mere lad and working for trifling wages in a cotton factory in Pawtucket, when a minstrel company visited the town. He was wild to attend, but the admission, 25 cents, was "not in sight"; and what should he do? Strolling along the street, his mind engrossed with the momentous problem, he encountered an old Irish woman who had just purchased an entire sheep at the butcher's and stood "wishing aloud" that she could find someone to carry it for her, and she'd pay 'em well fur it."

Here's my chance, thought Ben, and with the vision of the coveted "quarter" flashing through his mind, quickly offered his services. "Sure you're a foine gossoon, an' indade ye'll be well paid fur yer throuble," she said.

Thus assured, he shouldered the sheep, asking "How fur do you live ?" "Och, an' it's but a shtip or two, my shweet little mon, an' I wish' I was yer mither." Ben felt that he could carry the sheep all night for the dear old soul, but it was becoming rather heavy, and after going eight or ten blocks he ventured to ask: "Ain't we most there ?"

"Faith an' its jes' furninst us, darlin'," purred the old woman.

The "furninst," Ben found, was about half a mile further, when she stopped at her shanty and invited him in to "warrum" himself. No, no; though nearly frozen he'd no time to spare if he expected to get back to see the show; and he'd like to be paid. Whereupon the old woman thrust her hand into her capacious pocket, and, after fumbling in its depths for some time, finally brought forth a stick of candy, exclaiming, as she handed it to him: "There, take that, ye spalpeen; an' it's more'n ye desarve for takin' advantage of a poor old workin' woman"; and slamming the door in his face, Ben was certainly left out in the cold, and philosophically decided to forego his visit to the minstrels.

Ben, while relating this story, which he calls his first experience in minstrelsy, acknowledged that of all the vicissitudes encountered during his fifty years of show experience, this has endured in his memory as the bitterest; and that even now the very mention of sheep causes him a faintness.

Perhaps I should mention that to become a jig dancer was his earliest ambition, and the ability he early evinced in his heels was the pride and boast of Pawtucket. And this introduces another anecdote he enjoys relating, although it records another disappointment which befell him not long subsequently to his adventure with the Irish- woman and her sheep.

A minstrel show had reached his town with but meager assets, and with the company was a quite famous colored jig-dancer known as "The Boston Rattler." Even with this strong attraction (in early days a minstrel company was not complete without a good jig-dancer), the attendance was small, and the company found itself unable to meet its bills. As this would prevent their leaving, it was proposed 'that an extra effort should be made to draw out the people, and having learned of Master Bennie's home popularity as a dancer, a match was arranged between him and the "Rattler," to come off on the following evening. Ben was to receive ten dollars for his services, with the understanding that the "Rattler" should not "let himself out" in the dance, and that Bennie's popularity should not be disturbed. Small hand-bills announcing the event were well distributed, and resulted in packing the house. The Rattler kept his promise to "go easy," and the enthusiasm of the audience was unbounded when the decision was announced in favor of Bennie, who hurried home with the laurels of victory, although ashamed of part he had played in the deception—an emotion which he admits was considerably modified during his later years.

On the following morning, bright and early, Master Bennie called at the hotel for his "ten," and — the company had left town soon' after the performance!

Mr. Cotton was prominent not only as a fine banjoist, but—versatile, as were so many of the early players—an all-around comedian, dancer and "funny man," and an artist with the bones and tambourine.

His first engagement was in 1845, and with a side-show minstrel company connected with Van Amberg's Menagerie, associating with George Coes (later the California champion banjoist, whom I mentioned in a former number), who taught him "to pick out a few tunes on the banjo."

Closing with this company at the end of the season, he returned to his home with the determination to become a banjo player before engaging again. As before mentioned, banjos were scarce to be found in those days, and good ones were mostly of home-made construction; so, to secure one, he had either to make it or have it made, and as he had not been enriched to any appreciable extent through his side-show engagement, his choice was soon made, and he set about making one himself: the old story retold — the experience of nearly all the old-timers, my own as well.

Contrasting the conditions which beset our banjo pioneers in their pursuit of banjo knowledge with those which now obtain, the ease with which the players of to-day can equip themselves, not only with instruments to suit their most whimsical fancy, but printed music in great variety as well, I wonder, if the same conditions still obtained, would there now be so many banjoists? Hardly, I think. But the reflection is interesting.

Here is Cotton's experience as a banjo maker, given in his own words? —

"I couldn't come across a banjo, so I thought I'd try my hand at making one. I got an old sieve for the rim, and made a handle out of a stick of pine and whittled out some pegs of the same; then I got an old drum-head that had been thrown aside, soaked it all night. as it was hard and tough, and after several hours of hard work succeeded in stretching it over the rim and tacking it on : but when it was finished I was proud of it. But I soon got tired of it, having to heat it up every time I wanted to play; so I bargained with a friend of mine, in Pawtucket, who was quite a genius, to make one with screws on the rim to draw the head tight. The handle was a beauty—curly maple with smooth fingerboard; and oh, what a sweet tone it had!

I kept that banjo for several years, and got so I could play any number of jigs and banjo songs; but, as I had never learned music, it was a serious drawback to me. Finally I sold it for twenty dollars, and bought one of Wilson's silver-rim banjos; and I don't believe a finer-toned banjo has ever been put together." [*Wilson's very superior banjos were mentioned in the June number of* The Cadenza.]

In 1854 Cotton was with Matt Peel's Campbell Minstrels, the most popular traveling company on the road, then and until his (Peel's) decease many years later.

Hipe Rumsey was also with this company at the time—the primo banjoist. Ben had now become a good player, good enough— which implies much— to play for Master Tommy Peel, one of the best and most finished jig-dancers I ever knew, and who, before, had the orchestra for his dance. As a "danseuse" (wench dancer) Master Tommy's Lucy Long, in the little sketch bearing that name, displayed a versatility and mastery of his art that added greatly to his popularity.

In 1855 Cotton joined Sniffin's Minstrels, then located at 444 Broadway, New York, where, in addition to his banjo and other specialties, he introduced his version of the then famous character dance, "Essence of Old Virginny." It is generally understood that Frank Brower, one of the oldest and best delineators of the darkey, originated this highly characteristic dance, first calling it "Happy Uncle Tom." Later it was re-named "Essence of Old Virginny," by Tom Briggs, the banjoist, and has retained that title.

Cotton was one of the first to follow Brower, and was highly successful. Dan Bryant, then traveling through the West, also brought it out, and it became one of his strongest features. He first danced it in Galena, Ill., in 1855, to Ned Winchell's banjo. The dance portrayed an old plantation field-hand, so infatuated by music that when he heard it he became overpowered and was unable to restrain his impulse to dance; and in his ecstasy, oblivious of all else, he would labor with the clumsiest and most grotesque of steps, occasionally giving utterance to his joy in happy exclamations.

Brower had but few successful followers other than Cotton, Bryant, Newcomb, Arlington and, perhaps, Mart Sexton, who, however, excelled in nothing else; and when "made up" was the ideal personification of the clumsy, good-natured, happy plantation cotton-picker just out of the field, and in my estimation (I played for him while banjoist with Henry Woods' Minstrels, Broadway) was inimitable.

After filling his engagement with Sniffin's company, Ben and his best friend — his banjo — visited the South, where he engaged with the old circus managers, Spaulding and Rogers, on their little Mississippi steamboat, *The Banjo*, which, having been metamorphosed into a minstrel "hall," was devoted to "playing" the small towns and plantations located along the shallow bayous which could be reached in no other way. *The Banjo* was a little stern-wheeler with a big water-wheel, suggestive of an old saw-mill, clinging to its stern and splashing a veritable cascade when in motion. A calliope (steam piano) was a distinguishing and important feature of *The Banjo's* equipment.

Its function was to advertise the company. When nearing a landing at which it was intended to give a performance, it would be brought into action, waking the entire settlement and the surrounding country with its screeching; and nothing more in the way of advertising was necessary.

It didn't take long for it to become popular, for Frank Cardella, the pianist, and entire "orchestra" of the show, and who played it, knew well "The Hog-eye Man" and "Old Rackensack" — the "national anthems" of the section — and they sufficed to herald the coming of the "show folks" — an event in the lives of the isolated natives.

When visiting the plantations the "hall" would be literally packed with the colored slaves (for this was before our Civil War), the only whites attending being their owners who had given them this diversion, and who would stand at the ticket office, each checking off his own "niggers" as they passed into the hall, and paying for his "bunch"; and a happier or more demonstrative audience would be a rarity.

Ben availed himself of this opportunity for studying the characteristics of the Southern negro, often visiting the cotton fields, their cabins, attending their festivals, etc., and later, upon returning to the North, presented, as a result of his experience, his plantation scene of "Old Uncle Snow,' which quickly scored a success and equaling Frank Brower's "Essence" as one o the best representations of the genuine old darkey ever depicted on the stage.

A press article of the day gives the following interesting description of "Uncle Snow": "The strange pleasure which at first creeps and finally spreads over the old man's countenance, when the forgotten sounds of once-familiar strains strike his ear; the determination to leave when they abruptly stop, and his, inability to do so when they revive and overpower him, and his final abandoning himself to the song and dance, is a realistic and most forcible illustration of the powers of music on the susceptible Ethiopian !" Strong words, indeed, for our veteran, but deserving; and we may well honor him as one of the worthy pioneers of the banjo!

[ed.note: *Ben Cotton passed away in 1908, at the age of eighty. "New York, Feb 25 - They put one more of the real old time negro minstrels under the sod yesterday when they buried old Bed Cotton from Daniel Corbett's undertaking shop at 2 Manhattan Avenue....Ben Cotton was 80 years old when he died having been born in Pawtucket, R.I. in 1827. He was a pretty well-known character up in the New England town which he used frequently to visit....When Ben Cotton first got to be prominent in the minstrel profession, not long after the civil war ended, it was a great time for ballads about conflict and martial glory and that kind of thing. Such songs are "When the Cruel War is Over", and "Tenting on the Old Campground."*]

Harking back to the time when our banjo was in its infancy, and contrasting its then simple music with that of the present time, cannot but excite our wonder and astonishment at realizing how much has been accomplished since the days of Sweeney, Emmett, Pete Jenkins, Ned Winchell and the few other pioneers—the "first families" of the banjo who—some of them—still survive, living witnesses of the rapid development of its potentialities; a growth unparalleled in the history of any other musical instrument! And then, to think of the labors, the trials and vexations experienced by those old pioneers and their ambitious successors; their jealousies, rivalries, antagonisms! Yes, a battle royal has been waged all down the line—and now? Is it over? In the light of recent printed criticisms, I should say not, but with this remarkable difference, however: that while the same rancorous and antagonistic bitterness is still discernible, it seems now to be not the banjoists themselves who are the principal combatants, but their respective friends and partisans, whose opinions will ever remain the same, many of whom have never 'frayed" a string on the instrument.

But even so, what's the use? Must the instrument still stand alone the cause and representative of undignified strife? Why this pathetically pessimistic wail of "the passing of the banjo"?

And why this recent spasm of bitter criticism? I believe it to be true that the motives we are really actuated by are often quite different from those we suppose we are actuated by, and that opinion may sometimes outgrow even the scope of the instrument.

There are some whose heads are filled with noises that they mistake for musical thoughts; but a player needn't consider himself wronged simply because he cannot equal his superiors.

Common sense seems most uncommon with some, and when it ceases to perform its function, why, anything goes.

There never can be two equal players; a man has no duplicate. And where, indeed, would the players of to-day stand had others not gone before them and "blazed" the way? Why, Armstrong, Farland, Partee, Lansing, Lee and a few others have made all banjo players their debtors, the world over.

Apropos of the recent articles published in the *Sun*, I do believe that were the subject viewed dispassionately, the trouble would be found to lie not so much with our players, who have become "as thick as leaves in Vallambrosa," but in the millions of vile, disreputable imitations of the genuine banjo that are foisted continually upon the market by ignorant, unscrupulous and mercenary makers, and thus affording occasion for its most righteous disparagement in the estimation of musicians and the public generally. And the players must suffer! "Scolopax," whose recent letter to the *New York Sun*, excepting to the published criticisms on "The Passing of the Banjo," contains the following sensible advice: "If our devotees will but use good judgment in the selection of their music. pursue their labors artistically and fraternally, exercise their best efforts to improve the quality of tone in the instrument and show a neighborly disposition toward the brethren of their craft, we shall hear but little more of the "Passing of the Banjo."

As to the identity of "Scolopax," I would say that my acquaintance with him was formed over twenty years ago when he became my pupil, and that our relations of sincere and reciprocal friendship have continued to the present time. A gentleman of refinement and possessed of rare musical attainments, member of one of New York's most prominent and influential families and a successful Wall Street broker almost from his infancy, he has kept in touch with the banjo and its literature, and is an exceptionally brilliant executant in the banjo ("stroke") style of playing for which he has a preference.

[ed. note: The decline of the banjo's popularity was noted in a widely syndicated obituary of Frank Converse published in the fall of 1903, "The decline of the banjo followed soon after the public interest in minstrel

performances began to decrease. It is rarely heard on the stage now, even in vaudeville performances, and even the college clubs have lost their old enthusiasm for it. Now it is not even used to tie ribbons on."]

Banjo Reminiscences. VII

Written Exclusively for 'THE CADENZA. December 1901
BY FRANK B. CONVERSE, NEW YORK CITY.

During a recent conversation with one of the oldest minstrels I know, I was shown a clipping from an old number of Harper's Magazine in which Mr. Laurence Hutton essays to trace the history of Negro minstrelsy in America and succeeds in bringing together a large number of interesting facts in connection with early music and theatricals. I think the most surprising of his statements is one made on the authority of Mr. Charley White, one of our earliest Ethiopian comedians and minstrel managers, who, during his life, wrote much relating to minstrelsy and its members, and who, the article states, credits a Mr. Gottlieb Graupner, a German musician from Hanover, with being the 'father of negro song." He is said to have sung "The Gay Negro Boy," in character, *accompanying himself with the banjo*, at the end of the second act of "Oroonoko," on December 30, 1799, at the Federal Street Theatre, Boston; that Graupner settled in Boston in 1798, led the orchestra in the old Federal Street Theatre, kept a music shop, played the oboe, the double bass, and nearly every other instrument. I have omitted much of detail contained in Mr. Hutton's article, as irrelevant; but the general tenor lends the impression that he had familiar knowledge of his subject. But is it true? If so, it's a revelation to all with whom I ever have conversed about the banjo, and a wonder that so important an event could have slumbered so long. One hardly feels warranted in questioning so veracious an authority as Charley White, yet, in view of all that has been written relating to the first banjo, and by intelligent and capable historians contemporaneous with Mr. White and their unanimity of opinion respecting its creation at the hands of Joel Walker Sweeney, Mr. Laurence Hutton's statement, which does such violence to established tradition, unless supported by further and reliable corroborating, is, to express it mildly, extraordinarily improbable.

That all those who have written about the banjo and Sweeney, some of whom are intimately acquainted with the Sweeney family and "on the spot", so to speak, should have, by concerted action, conspired together to perpetuate a falsehood, seems incredible; and equally so that, within the range of my recollection at least, no other writer has risen to unmake accepted history.

The following extracts from a letter received by Mr. J. F. Henning, of Chicago, in 1890, from his friend, Mr. Geo. W. Inge, a gentleman broadly experienced and of unquestioned veracity, and who enjoyed an intimate acquaintance with the Sweeney family, will be read with satisfaction:

J. E. Henning, Esq.

"DEAR SIR I have just returned from my old home in Appomattox Court House, Virginia, the Birthplace of old Joel Sweeney, the inventor of the banjo. While there I visited a large number of his relatives, some of them now living at his old home; and also visited his grave. I gathered a few facts from old friends of his, as well as from his sisters. This information is reliable, coming as it does from responsible parties and from his own family. His full name was Joel Walker Sweeney, born about 1813, at his father's home, one mile northeast of Appomattox Court House, Virginia.

"The old original Sweeney, as far back as is known, was Moses Sweeney, grandfather of Joe and his brother, John Sweeney, both of whom owned large estates and valuable property in and around what is now Appomattox Court House, Virginia. My father owns the old Joe Sweeney property, lying one mile south of the Court House, while most of the Moses Sweeney property, lying one mile northeast of the Court House, is divided up into small tracts among the grandchildren.

"Old Joe had a number of brothers and sisters. Miss Martha, Miss Eliza, both now dead. Mary Jane married a Mr. Flowers, she is now a widow, and quite blind; about 70 years old, but retains her memory, is highly intelligent and full of information; I talked with her several times in relation to her brother Joe. Miss Lou Sweeney is dead. Her husband survives her and is living near the old home. The other sister, Bertha, married Allen Conner; they are living near the old home. The three brothers were: Joel Walker Sweeney, the eldest, born at the old home in 1813, died at the same place October, 1860, aged 47 years, and is buried in the old family burying-ground near his home; Richard Alex Sweeney, the next eldest, was a fine performer on the banjo and traveled with his brothers, Joe and Sam; he died in the latter part of 1859, in Washington, D. C., where he was buried by some of his friends. Sam Sweeney, the younger brother, was also a fine banjoist, and traveled with his brothers over the Eastern States. He was an attaché of General 'Jeb' Stuart's staff during our Civil War, when the General was killed. He then went with General Lee. He died at Orange Court House, where he was buried, in 1863.

'Old Joe was a fine performer on the violin. He and his brothers traveled extensively through the Northern and Eastern States. While traveling with Athon's Circus, he first conceived the idea of blacking face and hands and imitating the negro. The brothers having become proficient, visited Philadelphia and New York, where they gave a number of 'negro concerts,' as they called them. Athon claimed the distinction of being the originator of negro minstrelsy, but it is evident that Joe Sweeney, with his old banjo, first conceived the idea and put it into use.

"After concluding in New York, his brothers turned back, and Joe sailed for England, determined, if possible, to play his banjo before the Queen. In this he was successful, playing on several occasions for the Queen and members of the royal family. On his return he stopped at Lynchburg, Va. where he hired a carriage with four horses attached, and a driver, and drove to his old home, Appomattox Court House, twenty-five miles distant, in great style. After 'taking in' the neighborhood, he returned to Lynchburg and deposited $7,500 in gold—his remaining capital.

"It is very evident that Joe Sweeney was the father of negro minstrelsy as well as the inventor and perfector of the banjo. Several old and reliable farmers in Appomattox related to me how the negro slaves used to take a large gourd, attach a stick for a staff, and put on four strings made of horsehair, and how Joe would hang around with the negroes, learning their rude songs and playing an accompaniment on this rude instrument, and how he used to construct others, substituting a meal-sifter for the gourd. He finally made one, and getting hold of some strings, he put on a 'thumb-string,' as he called it, and very soon learned to play most any tune on it. This banjo was destroyed, and he then made another, a real banjo, making a number of improvements, and placed the fifth String.

"This was really his first perfect banjo, which he used for a number of years. In the meantime he had made banjos for his brothers, Sam and Dick, and they became fine performers."

Without doubt, the first female to play the banjo was one of Joe's cousins, Miss Polly Sweeney. Her brother Robert was a fine violinist. Being left-handed, the strings upon his violin were reversed. Miss Polly first essayed this instrument under her brother's instruction, and playing as he did—left-handed, although not so physically constituted; but later she chose the banjo and was taught to play by her cousin Joe. Her violin practice having confirmed the habit of left-hand playing, she preferred to continue it with the banjo, so Joe made a left-hand staff for the old rim. Mr. Inge states that "she became a fine performer, and that he had heard her play a great many times, and that she is still living (1890). She stopped playing a number of years ago and gave her banjo to a relative, a Mr. Durrum. He wanted to learn to play, but as it was left-handed he could do nothing with and threw it into an old closet where it remains to this day."

Mr. Inge secured this old instrument for his friend, Mr. Henning, and also much written testimony, verifying beyond question the facts that it was made by Joe Sweeney; that it is the first instrument to which he added the fifth string, and also the one upon which he first played in public.

I have extracted quite freely from Mr. Inge's letter, even to the extent of superfluity, perhaps; but it has seemed desirable to do so in verification of his long and familiar acquaintance with the Sweeney family, and, consequently, his ability to furnish a truthful story of the evolution of the first banjo.

To write of guitarists seems hardly within the range of banjo reminiscence, but as I have occasionally made departures from my subject to introduce what seemed would be interesting, and having been asked if I ever knew Tony Hernandez an old-time guitarist, and as I did know him well, for he and I were together with Matt Peel's minstrels, I trust a few words concerning him are acceptable to the reader.

Tony Hernandez, a Cuban, was, in any respects, a remarkable character. When he first became a professional I know not, but he was known in minstrelsy about 1855, and was then probably thirty-six or thiry-eight years of age.

My acquaintance with him began when we were members of Matt Peel's company. He claimed to have formerly been connected with the famous Ravel Pantomime troupe, which seems probable, for he was an excellent pantomimist, acrobat and gymnast.

In fact, he was a master of many accomplishments. He was a musical genius, and, though ignorant of the principles of music, was a fine guitarist, with most phenomenal fingers, and his solos were executed with a brilliancy and dash that captivated his audience.

He was an excellent flutist, and played that instrument in the "first part". He also played a horn in our brass band. But this was not the limit of his versatility. He was a ballet dancer *par excellence,* and his sketch entitled, "Dancing-master and Pupil," afforded him an opportunity for displaying his remarkable ability In this specialty, as well as his keen sense of burlesque.

He knew how to make all kinds of stage "properties," traps and trick settings, even shoes and dresses for stage wear; and how he could throw the knives!—long; heavy, spear-shaped blades; they must have weighed two pounds each—and he would hurl them in seemingly the most careless and reckless manner, yet with precision simply marvelous.

I well remember a little sketch in which he introduced this feat, for I was one of the assistants to hold a lighted candle near the target, and I have not forgotten the relief I experienced when he had finished without a mishap. Geo. W. ("Pony") Moore—then with our company, but later, and now, proprietor of Christy's Minstrels, London, England, would stand against a board background and be literally pinned to it with the heavy knives thrown by Hernandez, standing at a distance of fifteen or twenty feet away; no, not exactly standing, for he was continually "pirouetting" over the stage in the most grotesque of movements, and gesticulating wildly except when steadying himself for an instant and, with all his force, hurling the knife. The really, thrilling act was terminated by lodging a knife between each finger of Moore's outstretched hand, and then splitting an apple placed upon his head. Ned Winchell, who also held a candle in the act, used to say that what enabled Hernandez to succeed so well was the encouragement we gave him by our chattering Chinese comments.

Quite a romantic incident connected with his early life and exhibiting a phase of his dare-devil recklessness, is worth relating. It resulted from his association with the notorious filibuster, Walker, who was executed in Honduras in 1860, and whose adventures Hernandez had joined. In one of their raids he was captured, imprisoned and condemned to be shot. While in prison, having induced his guard to procure for him a guitar, he composed what he called his death song. It so happened that on the day preceding the one set for his execution the wife and daughter of one of the officials were visiting the prison, when they were attracted by the sounds of a guitar and the voice of Hernandez who, having observed them, began singing his mournful refrain. The pathos of the situation—a prisoner about to die calmly and resignedly chanting his own dirge—so impressed these sympathetic women that they hastened to the authorities and, pleading for his life, succeeded in securing a respite during which they successfully planned for his escape.

Hernandez, died in New Orleans, near the termination of our Civil War. He had retired from the stage, and for a few years preceding his death had engaged in teaching the guitar and flute.

Banjo Reminiscences. VIII

Written Exclusively for THE CADENZA. January 1902
BY FRANK B. CONVERSE, NEW YORK CITY.

Consistent with reminiscence, I have, so far, been looking backward, living again the Past in the congenial society of the old-timers and recalling as much of incident and experience relating to them as sluggish memory would revive.

So engrossing had this pleasant retrospecting become that a conviction seemed taking possession of me that all was the Past—that there was no Present. Happily, I have "come to" as it were, repelled the delusion and awakened to a realization that "there are others." Therefore, expressing an apology for having harped so continuously upon one string—a conclusion which doubtless has entered the minds of some of my readers—and promising to return to my favorite theme later, I will now undertake to vary the monotony by ringing up a new scene and introducing some "living pictures," representatives of the present, up-to-date period.

And of these up-to-daters, I sometimes am puzzled as to what the term really implies—a term seemingly so susceptible of a variety of interpretations. But is there no criterion, no standard to which this distinguishing appellation may be referred? Upon what basic principles or accomplishments may the aspiring artist safely predicate his assumption of being a full-fledged and thoroughly equipped up-to-dater?

Is it he who boasts of his familiarity with the old masters—Beethoven, Mendelssohn, Mozart, Liszt, or Wagner, Gounod, Rubinstein, Paderewski, et al.? Or the one familiar with his instrument, knows its utmost limits, capacity, powers and its shortcomings and rationally acquiesces to its legitimate, arbitrary sphere?

Certainly the banjo is neither a piano nor Sousa's Band, but an instrument limited to a range of but three octaves, at the utmost stretch of either finger-board or imagination, and while acknowledging its marvelous versatility, its inspiriting tone, high shading powers and susceptibility to modulation and most effective harmony, when under the control of dextrous fingers, to assume that the massive and intricate compositions of our great musical geniuses can, with but the rarest of exceptions be effectively, or even musically, rendered upon the instrument by never so expert executants is, as the lawyer would say, a presumption not supported by the facts.

But I do not wish to be misunderstood. This statement must in no respect be construed into a disparagement of the instrument. Certainly my well-known life-long attitude respecting it is a sufficient refutation of even the slightest inference in that direction. Nor would it be disparaging to either to compare mouse with an elephant. Each, within its environment, fulfills its life-work, its destiny; that and nothing more, and each would be subject to righteous ridicule were it to undertake to assume the functions of the other.

Just so the banjo versus, for instance, the piano.

Let us, for a moment, take a common-sense view of the instrument. Correctly speaking, it is an instrument bearing but four strings. The fifth or short string is not entitled to enumeration, as it can be but rarely stopped with advantage above the fifth fret, although its usefulness and necessity are well understood The four strings, when tuned, comprise but two musical fifths at the nut: but half the scale of either the violin or mandolin, and is still further abridged in comparison with the guitar.

Then consider the great length of the finger-board and the relatively great distances apart of but twenty-two frets, which must be distributed upon its entire length— from nut to rim, and consequently the impracticability of holding with the fingers chords of any considerable magnitude, and so often compelling an arpeggioed subterfuge when anything beyond is required, and which, of course, is "something different" and is not, in view of the old masters, a true interpretation. With the violin or mandolin, their finger-boards being short, with different tuning and so more comprehensive, these troubles do not obtain.

Then again, the instrument is limited to but one bass string, and which, as a bass of quality, is limited.

But it is unnecessary to pursue the analysis further. Every sensible banjoist possesses a clear understanding of the subject; however, it is a matter of surprise that despite the many restrictions, such wonderful results can be attained with the instrument—and legitimately! But there is a limit.

Of course our players are ambitious, aspiring and emulous to sustain the popularity of the instrument; but it has its own separate and distinct individuality and sphere which, though restricted, is what causes it to be a banjo, and when it is attempted to exceed these boundaries, its proprieties, it reminds me of Aesop's fable of the ox and the frog; the frog failed, you know.

To be sure, high-sounding titles of grand opuses alleged to be performed at banjo "recitals" look well on a program, give it tone, as it were; but the "artist," if he be a musician, or half a one, knows, back of his conceit, that he is dealing in misfits; that their true rendering on his instrument, minus a piano or orchestra, is a physical impossibility.

It is the opinion of many whom I know that to this playing under false pretences may be largely attributed the present and still growing apathy exhibited toward the instrument; not only among musicians, but lovers of the instrument generally; and, what is more, has tended to discourage those who, loving the instrument in its purity, would desire to learn it.

With our hyper-zealous banjo claimant what really happens? Why, a piano or an orchestra must come to the rescue, do all the playing, while the "virtuoso" struggles along as best he can with his "interpretation" of some grand opus or other until the agony is over, when, like the conceited fly on the wagon-wheel, who imagined it caused all the dust, he proudly exclaims, "See?" He graciously acknowledges the plaudits of his deluded audience. Well, that's one class of up-to-daters.

And then there are those whose quality of instruments and manner of execution excite the query whether the good old brilliant and sparkling banjo, with its rich, round, melodious and inspiriting tone, is not become obsolete, metamorphosed, reincarnated and taken on the airs and mannerisms of that musical "exquisite," the mandolin, which we captured from antiquated, somnolent Spain, and have developed its inherent beauties through the artistic ministrations of a Siegel, Pettine and Abt? But it is a mandolin—not a banjo— yet the appropriation of its tremolo by the latter is an invaluable acquisition, under judicious treatment. And there seems some measure of truth in this, for really honest, legitimate, full-souled banjos are about as rare as Cremona violins, and for a similar reason—smothered by "improvements."

And, do you know the history of the violin and its vicissitudes? Well, as it can be briefly told, and seems so *apropos*, I'll relate it. The violin assumed its present shape early in the seventeenth century, and although countless attempts have since been made to improve its construction, it not only remains without material change, but the oldest violins are esteemed the best. Neither the Stradivarius, Amati nor Guarnerius families of Cremona, and who were the creators of the instrument, knew the secret of its superiority. In fact, they were not possessed of any scientific knowledge or the laws of acoustics, and there seems some truth in saying that the instrument was a "divine inspiration."

The instrument quickly became popular and speedily found its way through the various countries. Upon reaching France it met with such high favor that it attracted the attention of the *savants* who, while recognizing its phenomenal powers, yet decided that as it was the creation of ignorant persons it certainly was not exactly what it should be, needed to be "improved," and that they were the proper ones to attend to the matter. So they met in solemn conclave, put their heads together, and caused to be constructed an instrument in accordance with their particularly advanced ideas and all the laws of acoustics that could be brought to bear upon the subject, and—well----it was pretty—looked fine, but, strange to discover, lacked one rather important feature— tone! So they displayed their wisdom by concluding to drop the subject from any further consideration. That's all. I merely relate it as an instance of history repeating itself as exemplified in the life of the banjo and its "scientists."

But to resume: I have lately had correspondence with some of our players, and as it afforded me some pleasure, it may not be uninteresting to the reader, and, so minded, I will submit some liberal extracts from these letters.

And first, it affords me pleasure to refer to one, whose light has, by no means, been hidden under a bushel—Mr. Vess Ossman. This gentleman is not only eminently distinguished in a general way, but specially as having been identified with the phonograph for many years, and the disseminator of banjo music through that channel, which has been of inestimable value to the instrument in thus spreading the glad tidings all over the globe.

When but a little boy he evidenced a passionate taste for the instrument, and acquiring a good knowledge of the principles of music nearly at the outset, was enabled to study the instrument intelligently. To his genuine love for the banjo, his assiduous, painstaking analysis and study, is to be attributed the exalted position he has attained. A genius as well as brilliant executant, his facility in shading and technique enables him to portray his pieces with startling fidelity. One great charm of his playing is his wonderful ease, and the grace and perfection of his style have won him thousands of admirers, and gone far to sustain and popularize the instrument.

Banjo Reminiscences. IX
Written Exclusively for 'THE CADENZA. February 1902
BY FRANK B. CONVERSE, NEW YORK CITY.

Continuing with Mr. Ossman, and referring to his appearance in London, England, in the occasion of Essex and Cammeyers Banjo Concert, May 10, 1900, he writes:

"Believing, from the flattering public announcements, that great things were expected of me, and never having felt the pulse of an English audience, I underwent a slight mental disturbance, and unfortunately chose for my opening one of those heavy selections familiarly distinguished as an 'op.' The work of an eminent foreign musician.

"While it was well received, yet the applause seemed lacking that solidity and hearty appreciation so easy to recognize and so assuring to a performer. It seemed more of a sympathetic commiserating nature, as if saying: 'Poor fellow! - and just to think of his journeying three thousand miles just for that!' So I interpreted it, and concluded I had not produced the 'lost chord' they were expecting; and so, on recall, I changed tactics, risking my arrangement of 'Bunch of Rags,' and it seemed as though Bedlam had broken loose. I had struck the responsive chord, and the recalls that followed drew heavily on my repertoire."

Of Mr. Ossman's repertoire, which includes the popular "opuses," overtures, "Carmen," "Poet and Peasant," "William Tell," Moszkowski's dances, Chopin, "Hungarian Rhapsodies by Liszt, etc., etc., melodramatized to the capacity of the instrument, he naïvely says: "Why, I need them in my business, as it is necessary, you know, for a professional to cater to all sorts of tastes and intelligences, though, as a rule, my arrangements of our popular American composers are best received by our audiences."

Mr. Ossman was a lustrous star in the brilliant galaxy of our representative artists assembled at the Grand Banjo, Mandolin, and Guitar Festival Concert given at Boston Jan 22: an epoch—marking event in the history of these instruments.

In April next Mr. Ossman is to appear again in London, at Clifford Essex's Banjo Concert; following which event he will accept an engagement at the 'Empire,' the finest music hall in London.

It may savor of vanity, but pardonable, I trust in one who has ever been ready to assist a learner, to clip the following from one of Mr. Ossman's letters: "You may not be aware of it, but to you I owe a great deal. Your banjo arrangements, furnished me at the time I was learning the banjo, were my ideal, and anything with the name of Converse attached to it was 'good enough for me'"

Mr. Ossman was born at Hudson, N.Y. Aug 23, 1868, and possessed his first banjo at the age of twelve years. It was a home made affair, built by a candymaker in the same town, who had some knowledge of the instrument, and from whom young Ossman received his first ideas in a course of ten lessons—"simplified method."

At the expiration of this "course" he had excelled his teacher, which progress so interested his father that he decided he should receive proper instruction, and to that end he engaged the services of the leader of the orchestra of the opera house, Joe Kelly, who Ossman says, "was a good old soul and dearly loved the banjo."

With Kelly he started with the rudiments, memorized his first scale, and began his real work.

He remained with his teacher one year, receiving three lessons a week, and advanced so rapidly that at the expiration he "could read and play anything published in the banjo books of that time."

His popularity extended rapidly, and his services were constantly sought for parties, dances, concerts, even the church sociables; all of which he says was good for me, made me enthuse all the more." Continuing, he says: 'I then began to purchase banjo books and music, got a good banjo, and then the practice—how I *did* go at it. Fourteen hours a day was nothing. And many an hour did I put in on your 'Devil's Dance,' which selection, by the way, would be a good thing for the up-to-date banjoists to look over, who put 'op.' to their selections on their programmes.'

"All this time my father kept a bakery in the town, and I drove the delivery wagon. and, I assure you, everyone in the place knew Vess and his banjo, and to that I attribute the success of *our* bakery.

"About 1886, E. M. Hall visited our town with a minstrel show. I soon made his acquaintance, and we frequently played together. About the same period banjo tournaments were taking place along the river towns. Of course I had to put in an appearance, and was fortunate enough to win all the first prizes.

"Having learned that a grand banjo tournament was to came off at Chickering Hall, New York, introducing some of the most prominent players, I, at Mr. Hall's suggestion, and assurance — 'go ahead, and you will win' — decided to participate. Well, I went, a stranger among them, and, to my surprise (having learned that the affair was not to be *bona fide*, that the prize-winners had been decided upon), I was awarded the second prize. Ruby Brooks, of course, received the first prize.

"However, it affords me much pleasure to state that my first piece elicited most enthusiastic approbation, which assured me greatly; and I followed with John M. Turner's 'opus' of 'Pretty Little Queen,' which was the recipient of equal demonstrative favor. You must remember that I was playing the plain, unadulterated banjo, with no piano-solo attachment (as with the others), and the favor I received from the audience assured me that they were all the better pleased for it. And this was my advent in the City of New York."

I regret that want of space precludes a more extended mention of Mr. Ossman, whose brilliant career furnishes so worthy an example for the encouragement of others. Suffice it to say that he has worked for what he has attained. In addition to his professional engagements here and abroad he has for the past twelve years supplied our best phonograph companies with their finest banjo music. He was also honored by being selected as the banjo-soloist *par excellence* of America at the National Export Exposition in Philadelphia, Pa. A player whose execution, remarkable for its perfect clearness, with a repertoire practically inexhaustible, he displays a genius in adjusting the most elaborate admissible compositions to the unique capacities of the instrument. In view of what he has accomplished with the banjo, it is deemed not too extravagant to say that Mr. Ossman stands today the foremost, representative of his school.

Way down in Texas, within the confines of San Antonio, there quietly dwells and labors in the musical vineyard one of most modest mien, but one whose fame has gone throughout the land, and though not illumined by the footlight's glare, rests upon a surer, more imperishable foundation — the players and teachers he has developed; and his name is Charles S. Mattison.

Hidden in this far-away section of our country, as if seeking seclusion, yet his grand work has shone forth like a radiant star, and his studio has long been a veritable Mecca for the devotees and seekers for banjo truths.

The gentleman was born in New York City, in 1838, near the present location of *The Cadenza*. Bereft of parents when an infant, he found a home with an aunt residing on a plantation in Alabama, where, as he says, he "spent his happy childhood with little darkey playmates; and to slip off after supper to the negro 'quarters' and listen to their quaint, crude music and watch their dancing was my delight. When old enough to visit a colored barbecue, where I first heard a fiddle, I nearly went wild with delight, and many a crude attempt I made at fiddle-making, purloining my aunt's silk and flax for strings.

"When about five years of age, we moved to Tuscumbia, Alabama, for school facilities, and I soon possessed a real fiddle a cheap affair, to be sure, little better than a toy, but I managed to scrape out the negro airs I had so often listened to. About this time there came along a negro trader with a gang of slaves, one of whom carried a banjo which he could 'thumb right smart,' they said; and so I thought, for, whether it was his playing—which was crude, of course—or the inspiriting tone-quality of the instrument, I was captivated, and determined to own a banjo as soon as circumstance would admit. But the realization of my fond hope was baffled, for I was sent North to Poughkeepsie, N. Y., and placed in school. However, I was not without music, and was permitted to receive violin instruction under a most competent teacher. Although left-handed, my teacher insisted at first on my bowing with my right, but chancing to discover me using my left hand, and observing that my execution was much better, he permitted me to continue, and I became known as 'the fiddler who played over the bass.'

"But to be brief, wearying of school, my mind turned to the sea, and I embarked on a clipper ship engaged in the China tea trade. A long and tedious four years' voyaging having cooled my ardor for the sea, I returned to the South, settling in Holly Springs, Miss. Business calling me to Memphis, Tenn., where you were then teaching the banjo (1858), I soon sought your studio and that was a banner day for me—a new revelation of the banjo, and it didn't take you and me long to arrange terms for lessons, and now, as I recall the incidents of a somewhat varied past, it is truth to say that that meeting with you in Memphis was the shaping of my subsequent life and profession; and I feel that to the thorough foundation so ably inculcated by your teaching, writings and influence, I owe whatever of proficiency and knowledge of the banjo I may have acquired."

At the time of our Civil War, Mr. Mattison resided at Holly Springs, and naturally imbibed the political sentiments of the South. In the regiment to which he was attached were many of his musical friends who formed a little musical coterie, appointing him their leader. When starting for the "front," the citizens presented to them a variety of instruments, which, he says, "proved a joy to them in their camp life, but brought a grief when the strings gave out and no more to be had in the Confederacy.

"From dampness in tenting, the violin soon fell to pieces, and the last glimpse I had of my banjo was when we were toiling up the steep and rugged Clinch Mountain in Tennessee; the individual who was carrying it, disgusted with its dilapidated condition, and chancing to pass an old darkey trudging down the mountain, hung its headless rim upon his neck and it was soon lost to sight."

Upon returning from the war, Mr. Mattison found his affairs in such a state that he was reduced to the necessity of seeking any employment he could obtain for the support of himself and family, teaching when opportunity offered. Finally, leaving Holly Springs, he resided and taught in several Southern cities until about twenty years ago he had drifted to San Antonio. Here he found his haven. Meeting with most substantial success at the very beginning, and encouraged by the patronage of the most prominent families, he decided to become a Texan. A wise conclusion, truly, for, from then to now, he has been prosperous in his profession, is the resident teacher at one of the principal colleges, has a large clientage among the fashionable and influential families, and further varying his labors by occasional professional public engagements and proudly boasts the assertion that he has "developed more talented and finished players and teachers than perhaps any other teacher in the Southwest." Mentioning scores of his pupils, ladies and gentlemen, many of whom are prominently identified with the stage, some serving professionally in colleges and other musical institutions in Texas and other States, he specially recalls Con Boyle as one of his favorite proteges, who visited New York a few years since, and whose remarkable proficiency as a banjoist was quickly recognized by our players.

It is a regret that his stay was brief——so excellent a representative and teacher, but illness compelled his return to San Antonio, where, after a brief illness, he ceased to be. Louis Schuetze is another whose artistic and refined execution has earned him an enviable position in the banjo world; and Mitchell Mathison, who stands upon the same plane; also one to whom he alludes as "his friend as well as pupil"—Fred Gerrish, now associate teacher with A. A. Farland in New York, of whom Mr. Mattison writes: 'He came to me a number of years ago to learn the banjo and, discovering he was specially endowed with musical talent, I decided at the very beginning to put him at hard, dry, technical study. I remember how he rebelled, but finally yielded to persistence, and his advancement was remarkably rapid; and I do believe that for thoroughness and proficiency, his superior is rare to be found."

A strong assertion, verily, but then it's Mattison who utters it. Mr. Mattison's children, a son and three daughters, come honestly by their musical talent, and are proficient on various instruments. His son enjoys more than local fame as a teacher and professional banjoist, and, especially, one of his daughters—Mrs. Jennie McDonald—is not only known as an artistic player, but as the possessor of a fine voice, and her happy rendering of the popular songs of the times.

So near the completion of my sketch, and I have mentioned only Mr. Mattison's banjoistic attainments; but happily it is permitted me to do further justice to the gentleman by a mention of his violinistic ability and his high professional standing as player and teacher of that "king of instruments," even though he does "play over the bass." But whether he excels most in his mastery of the mandolin, is a question. However, so much I have taken pleasure in writing of a scholar, musician and gentleman.

Banjo Reminiscences. X
Written Exclusively for THE CADENZA. March 1902
BY FRANK B. CONVERSE, NEW YORK CITY.

"There is a massive book published in New York City, in the preparation of which the energetic and painstaking publishers aided by a corps of experts, have spared neither time, labor nor expense, and have produced, doubtless, the most exhaustive compilation of useful and invaluable biographical information extant.

"Should I inform you that this stupendous enterprise originated from a purely altruistic emotion of benevolence and love for our fellow-man, I fear I would be misunderstood did I not further explain that said love excitation received its impulse from a psychical diagnosis of fellow man's willingness, under certain conditions, to separate himself from his lucre. However overlooking any little idiosyncrasy of that kind, I conscientiously recommend the book, as it will be found to contain brief but concise mention of all the prominent celebrities of the city. And right here, and despite my constitutional modesty, candor compels me to say that during many successive years of its publication 'John M. Turner, Banjoist,' has been a conspicuous legend in its pages. The biography, unavoidably brief for want of incident, omits nothing, however, of any particular interest to anyone; but if your facile pen can derive any inspiration from the 'sketch,' why, dilate, fill in the details, and I'm 'It.' You'll find the book in most any drugstore or business place, generally secured by a chain. Ask the man to let you see it."

Thus facetiously replied John M. Turner upon being solicited for incidents of his life. Not much, truly, for one so long and prominently identified with the banjo as one of its most brilliant lights! But the gentleman has lived a life; hence the query whether reticence may be a sufficient excuse for such excessive modesty, such self-abnegation or, if from pure contrition of conscience, he would plead guilty to the fact? This I am unable to answer. However, evasion cannot, for history's sake, be allowed to avail, and, thanks to a long and intimate acquaintance with the gentleman, I possess considerable *ante-mortem* data.

In view of much that must have happened — which belongs to oblivion, for the reason above explained — Mr. Turner's oft- repeated statement that he "took to the banjo naturally when but a lad" must be taken for granted, and will, I believe, be generally credited; though he says, his first knowledge of music was not gained from that instrument. Quoting from his letter, his "only musical instruction was acquired through lessons on the piano and violin, and, when I took up the banjo, following your system of instruction and studies; and when sufficiently advanced, I made my own arrangements, transcribing such selections as pleased me from piano and violin music."

During several years preceding his professional advent he was engaged in manufacturing sashes and blinds, which, though highly lucrative, was far from congenial to a person of his aesthetic taste and inclination; and, meeting with a severe accident from too close an affiliation with one of his buzz-saws (vide old saying) which nearly severed his left arm, he relinquished the business and devoted his energies to his favorite musical studies.

And here occurs another lapse, during which he and his banjo were occasionally in evidence at amateur affairs, benefits and social entertainments, so maturing the foundation of his future success; but his first professional engagement was in connection with John K. Buckley, appearing with this gentleman in duet and meeting with much popular favor. After a few successful seasons, this association was severed, each deciding to paddle his own canoe.

From then to the present time, Mr. Turner has actively followed his profession, which has led him all over the globe—nearly; and, when not before the footlights, his philanthropy has been exercised in teaching the young idea how to "pick."

A distinguishing feature of Mr. Turner's playing, other than his wonderful command of technical skill and fine regard for artistic symmetry, is his introduction of, I might say, some startling effects, for which, however, he finds excuse in saying that he "found them useful to enliven the interest of his audience," and so he "made it a specialty to introduce a variety of tricks between Mendelssohn & Co. and Old Virginny Reels."

He claims to have originated banjo "juggling" — the truth of which assertion I entertain not the shadow of a doubt, for I've never seen it successfully duplicated by those who have essayed it — manipulating three, and sometimes four, banjos at the same time; and judging from the remarkable dexterity he displays in controlling them, it could hardly excite additional astonishment were he to increase their number.

Referring to the act, he explains that he did not "juggle or otherwise subvert banjo playing as a display of superior ability, or for any particular pleasure or satisfaction, but because it took better and amused certain audiences when they seemed dull and unappreciative of legitimate banjo playing;" and he finds ample excuse in saying that "any merchant not having marketable commodities in any line had best keep out of business or he'll be out of it." He amusingly adds, "Having thereby acquired a reputation as a juggler instead of a player, I then introduced such trifles as overtures, 'Zampa,' 'Poet and Peasant,' Gounod's 'March Funebré,' a few Chopins or Paderewskis to vary the monotony."

Mr. Turner's abilities as a composer have received the most flattering recognition from our musical critics, and many of his compositions, among which may be mentioned "The Minstrel's Patrol," "Pretty Little Queen" and "Cake-walk Jubilee," have become standards in the repertoires of our most famous banjoists. And if additional fame were gratifying it lies in the legion of players and teachers who have graduated from his studio, for the past twenty or more years located at 1307 Broadway, New York, and only recently abandoned upon the demolition of the building in the march of improvements.

As a fitting ending of this sketch, I append the following clipping, from an old paper, relating to Mr. Turner:

"John M. Turner, who is, perhaps, the only banjoist who has played in every city of importance in Great Britain, Germany, France, Italy and the United States, tells an amusing story of his first appearance in Glasgow, at the Scotia Music Hall, some few years ago. During the rehearsal the leader, Sam Tute, in a fraternal spirit told Turner that it was customary for every artist to make an announcement to the audience of what he or she intended to do. Turner consequently, at his debut, announced, in his loudest voice, that his first selection 'would be the famous "Turkish Patrol," made popular in the United States by the greatest of American bandmasters, P. S. Gilmore; also throughout Great Britain by Dan Godfrey,' and called special attention to the effects or imitations of a band approaching from a distance and dying away as they marched past and receded. "He then took his seat, and after playing the preliminary soft effects that the distance required, was surprised by a general shout all over the theatre: "Louder! Louder!"

"Turner, not heeding the interruption, thought that by persistency he could weather the storm and hurry the Turks' band to its *fortissimo*, but his nonchalance seemed to exasperate the audience, so that 'Louder' and 'Hurry up' was too much to stand. So, without stopping, but signaling the orchestra to stop (tacit), Turner determined to fight it out alone. Holding up one hand to the audience to keep quiet, and still playing with the other (his playing not having ceased whatever since his first note was struck), he buckled into the first jig that came to his mind, and jig after jig, Scotch and Irish, followed with all the spirit of leading a forlorn hope. The audience at once, hearing their old familiar airs jerked out of an instrument new to them at the time, were fairly wild with enthusiasm, and kept time to the music with feet, voice and hands. After about thirty jigs had been played, he arose and left the stage, bathed with perspiration, accompanied by the approving shouts of the audience and shrieks of laughter from the musicians in the orchestra. On his encore he announced that 'he never would play the "Turkish Patrol" again without hiring a hall in advance and explaining to the Glasgowites by means of a stereopticon or panorama what the Turks really were trying to do on this particular occasion.' After the performance, a gentleman, Mr. Edwards, came around to the stage-door and asked Turner, how it was that a string of Irish jigs came to be called the 'Turkish Patrol.' Turner immediately explained that in America, Irish longshoremen were called by the vulgar appellation of Turks, and as they unloaded vessels carrying *petroleum* and sang jigs at the same time, the combination was euphonized. Hence we have the name 'Turkish Patrol.'

Banjo Reminiscences. XI
Written Exclusively for 'THE CADENZA. April, 1902
BY FRANK B. CONVERSE, NEW YORK CITY.

Among the many good things teeming in last month's issue of *THE CADENZA*, I would like briefly to refer to its able and highly interesting sketches, with "photos" of some of the officers, the founders of the New American Guild of Banjoists, Mandolinists and Guitarists, through whose personal, indefatigable exertions the Guild has risen into most substantial being. Yes, it has become a fact, and now it's easy to praise; but it's my opinion that too much of this latter cannot be bestowed upon its founders, Partee, Morris, Farland, Lansing, Seigel, Odell, Kitchener and a few others, through whose earnest zeal the undertaking has been accomplished. Indeed, the entire musical fraternity is to be congratulated upon the far-reaching benefits which are sure to accrue to each individual one as a result of their labor. And purely a labor of love it has been for them—no pecuniary expectations to be realized, but actuated solely by enthusiasm and an ambition to exalt and dignify not alone the instruments, but their teachers and representatives as well. Really, ladies and gentlemen of the musical profession, we should doff our hats (ladies wear hats, I believe) to these gentlemen in thankful recognition of their invaluable service for the protection and countless other benefits which this organization assures for all time to come.

Referring to Mr. Lansing, I have recently had the pleasure of a very interesting correspondence with the gentleman, and, though Editor Partee wrote many pleasant things about him in the number referred to, still I cannot resist the inclination to extract freely from one of his letters to me, even though he was pleased therein to mention me most kindly. He writes:

"I have read your articles with much pleasure, and as I've always spoken of you and considered you the

Autocrat of the Banjo, I have naturally agreed with you on such matters as you refer to in your last one in *THE CADENZA* (January). I consider your 'Fawn Mazurka,' 'Aurora Gallop,' etc., to be the height of banjo arrangements. They *fit* the instrument and are musical. I like some of the standard works, such as the 'Bolero,' by Moszkowski, and a few others which do not become simply burlesques by putting them on the 'jo'; but I do not care to hear overtures which demand forty or fifty orchestral instruments for a proper rendition. I believe in advancing, but there is enough good music within the reach of all if they would but accept the banjo in its proper sphere, and not try to emulate the so-called virtuosos.

"Now, as to my autobiography, I don't know that I can say very much of any general interest, but from the following you may cull something: I was first attracted to the banjo by hearing George Swayne Buckley play. That was in 1874. I was then fourteen years of age, and was living in Wareham, Mass. I had been well drilled in music on piano and organ, but after hearing the fascinating tones of the banjo, I thought of nothing else until I possessed one. It was worth about fifty cents, I guess. The head was tacked on, and I always had to hold it over a lamp to tighten it." (The old, old story—the trials that tested enthusiasm and patience!) I remember once trying a thick paper head while waiting for a new one from

Boston. Of course the paper head was a failure, but I was inexperienced then.

"My second banjo had six brackets, and was considered quite a 'plunk' for those days, in my town. My third banjo was supposed to be loaned to me, and thereby hangs a tale.

"A gentleman particularly fond of the banjo. and who thought I was a wonder, bought the banjo in Boston and gave it to his wife. He thought he must do this— slightly hen-pecked, perhaps—as he had to account to her for every dollar he spent, she having a small fortune and he nothing but pleasing ways. Well, I suppose she thanked him for this evidence of his love, etc., and—laid it carefully away. About a week later he discovered where it had been placed, and brought it to me to try, and with me it remained, he forgetting (?), whenever he called, to take it home. I think I used it nearly two years. At that time I was a clerk in a drug store, and I recall many pleasant evenings I passed in playing for the boys.

"In 1878 I came to Boston, taking a position as prescription clerk in a drug store in East Boston. I continued practicing faithfully on the 'jo,' buying everything I could find in the line of banjo books and music. I have now, somewhere at home, one of your methods, which I bought about that time.

"In 1879 I made the acquaintance of the late S. S. Stewart, whose friendship continued up to the time of his death. In the spring of 1883, I dropped the mortar and pestle and began teaching. The fact that I have been at it ever since shows that I then struck my proper vocation and if further evidence were necessary to convince me that the occupation has been very pleasant and agreeable, physically as well as mentally, I might add that when I left the drug business I weighed 127 pounds, and now tip the scales at 195!

"In 1883, Mr. A. D. Grover and I organized the Boston Ideal club, which organization has played from Maine to California and from British Columbia to Florida. This is the only Banjo Club that ever covered the Continent in a professional way.

"Your mention of the popular banjoist, E. M. Hall, and his artistic attainments is a most worthy tribute to a most brilliant performer, and I most decidedly share your opinion. He has been a very particular friend of mine for the past fifteen years; and I am proud to say that today I can count among my friends about all the banjoists of both the old and the new schools."

I am happy to be able to agree with Mr. Lansing in his opinion, of P. C. Shortis, a banjoist who has, indeed, made a most enviable record. Several years ago I listened to his playing for nearly two hours, and marveled at his brilliant execution. Mr. Lansing says: "P. C. Shortis called on me a few days ago, and entertained me with his inimitable style of playing, and I am of your opinion in regard to the 'characteristic' music being the proper kind for the banjo."

As Editor Partee has so truthfully said, in writing of Mr. Lansing in last month's issue of *THE CADENZA*, "we might write at length of Mr. Lansing's many achievements, but he is so universally known," etc.; but, even so, doubtless such an undertaking would fall far short of what Mr. Lansing could relate were he to become his own historian ; and it is to be hoped that, if but for the encouragement of all who are striving for the mastery of some instrument, the inspiration may come upon him to discover the "royal road" — if there be one — to the eminence he has attained.

Not alone as an executant is Mr. Lansing famous, but as a composer and arranger for the banjo, also the guitar and the mandolin, he stands with the most popular authors of the day; and knowing well the capacities of his favorite instruments. His compositions and arrangements, which have reached the proportions of volumes, are recognized favorites wherever the instruments are known ; and we shall never hear of "the passing of the banjo" so long as we have a Lansing to shape its music.

Banjo Reminiscences. XII

Written Exclusively for THE CADENZA. May, 1902
BY FRANK B. CONVERSE, NEW YORK CITY.

In the last issue of *THE CADENZA* (April) I was afforded the pleasure of presenting a brief sketch of Mr. Geo. L. Lansing; one, however, whose eminent position in the musical world hardly required an attempt at eulogy from my pen but, through correspondence, possessing much which I deemed of general public interest pertaining to the life and experiences of this world-famed artist, I was induced to record it in the columns of our representative magazine— *THE CADENZA.*

Although occupying so exalted a position as does Mr. Lansing, we are not oblivious of the fact—which in no sense, however, detracts from it— —that there are others of whom we may proudly boast. Those who have contributed to the grand total have added lustre to the brilliant galaxy of our representatives of the banjo, mandolin and guitar; and prominently among these must be recognized Mr. Wm. S. Baxter, the popular teacher of these instruments, who for many years has been their representative in Chicago, Ill. It has been a highly esteemed privilege to have long enjoyed a pleasant correspondence with the gentleman, who, at my solicitation, has furnished me with the following sketch of his experiences, which I believe will be appreciated by the readers of The Cadenza:

"Chicago, March 12, 1902.

"My Dear Mr. Converse:

"I have been doing jury service during the past two weeks, which may partially account for silence. I owe you an apology for seeming neglect, which I herewith take pleasure in offering. Your request caused me to cudgel my memory into a partially submissive condition, whereby I find but few incidents that might interest readers of THE CADENZA; in fact, I might sum my life up in a few words, viz.: "At a very early age I was born, and am still here." Commonplace, true, but nevertheless a fact; however, I shall briefly try and outline a few of the details of my existence to date, and hope that your never-failing imagination and fertile fancy, together with your more than facile pen, may develop a spirit of interest. Some years ago I had a congenial (I hope) correspondence with Mr. John M. Turner, and was much pleased with his quaint wit and the droll manner of expressing himself. I see from the nature of his biography in The CADENZA that he still seems surcharged with the same spirit of fun and facetiousness. Better so than the soul of a grouch, say I. Well, my dear Mr. Converse, I am sensible, fully, of the honor you would do me, and am afraid the material you will have to work with will be inadequate to bring about a successful or satisfactory result. Should it be so, all praise must go to the builder in the meantime, permit mc to thank you for the courtesy, and offer you my sincere good wishes.

Cordially yours,

William S. Baxter.

"I was born in Cincinnati, Ohio, during the second year of the late Civil War. Upon the return of my father, who was an officer in the Union ranks, we took up our residency in Kentucky, where we lived a rural life, placid, uneventful and pastoral. I might say the brightest and happiest days of my life were spent in the hills and meadows of the Blue Grass region. The first recollection I had of a banjo was one made by a neighbor who entranced me with his songs and rude playing. The instrument was 'homemade' - hickory neck, cheese box rim, hand whittled pegs, tack-head, etc. (no doubt you have seen such as I here describe briefly). That banjo and the player inspired in me a never-to-be-forgotten desire to learn to play, and as I grew older, when I reached the age of fourteen, I possessed myself of a modern (?) banjo with a metal rim, walnut neck and all the trimmings which were then considered necessary. We were at this time again residents of Cincinnati, and I applied myself persistently, with efforts worthy of a better cause, to perfect myself in the art of banjo manipulation. I became what was considered a boy prodigy, and appeared in concert many times with more or less success. In the meantime I worked at the guitar, violin and cello—spasmodically, 'tis true, but succeeded in eventually acquiring a partial proficiency, but never permitted my loyalty to my first *love* to become alienated.

"I traveled considerably in a professional capacity, but *could not* reconcile myself to the roving life, and eventually wended my way back to my home and family, when I went manfully to work in the effort to equip myself for the occupation which I have followed with a reasonable degree of success, both pecuniarily and artistically, even up to the present time. It has been my pleasure and good fortune to have met and communed musically with nearly all of the famous banjoists during the past twenty years, among whom might be mentioned E. M. Hall, Wm. A. Huntley, John M. Turner, I.P.C. Shortis, C. E. Dobson, E. C. Dobson, Billy Carter, Sam Devere, Ed. French, G. L. Lansing, Tommy Glynn, Mays and Hunter, A.A. Farland, Brooks and Denton, as well as most of the well known makers of banjos, but regret to say that he whom I felt largely indebted to for inspiration, encouragement, as well as information, was known to me only by reputation —- -none other than yourself. I studied your books, methods and arrangements, and learned much to my advantage. I became attached to a college of music in Cincinnati, and remained there in the capacity of head of the Department of Banjo, Mandolin and Guitar until 1886, when I felt that I might find a larger and better field for my work elsewhere so, in consequence, I chose Chicago and I never regret having made the change, as I have been more successful here than I feel my efforts justify. The incidents associated with my professional career would, I fear, prove commonplace and uninteresting to readers of *The Cadenza* chiefly for the reason that they savor only of a local flavor, and I cannot flatter myself that I am known to the great array of musicians who are interested in instruments loved by us all. There is one incident connected with my life, and that of recent occurrence, the memory of which will always remain with me. And that was the meeting of our well-beloved President McKinley and his most charming wife, who were visiting at the home of relatives here, who were pupils of mine. I received an invitation to spend an evening with the family, and was received cordially and graciously by both the President and his wife. I played for them all evening. and, upon departing, Mrs. McKinley presented me with a huge bunch of roses. With a charmingly given invitation to visit them again. I did so later in the week, and received from her own hands a photo of both the President and herself, with autographs. These are now my most cherished and valued possessions. I merely mention these occurrences incidentally. They would not, perhaps, be of interest to *The Cadenza*.

I really fear I am an indifferent biographer of self, for my temperament is rather inclined toward diffidence, and for that reason my personal trumpet must be poorly blown. However, I must beg that you will do for me that which Mr. Turner requested of you, to use *your* imagination and other valuable requisites, in which event the biography of the subscriber must needs be interesting, even though he gave you but little material to work upon. Personally I affect golf (simply for the exercise), ride horseback quite a little in summer, am a dog crank (own three), have many faults, a few doubtful virtues, am five feet eleven inches in height, weigh two hundred pounds (net), gray hair (premature, my friends say), and have been a member of the B. P. 0. E. for many years, as well as a "Shriner" in the thirty-second hole of Masonry. Now, I think that covers the territory pretty clearly, and it remains for you to use the pruning-knife as well as the blue pencil. Perhaps you may work out a column. If the story does not appear, I shall know that my life was hardly worth the taking, and in consequence must seek another resting-place than in *The Cadenza* Sarcophagi.

Banjo Reminiscences. XIII

Written Exclusively for THE CADENZA. June, 1902
BY FRANK B. CONVERSE, NEW YORK CITY.

Reflecting upon the published tributes to the departing old-time minstrels which have appeared so frequently of late must occasion some surprise that so many lights of early minstrel days have still been flickering unobserved in our midst, and force the conclusion, not that minstrelsy is still dying out but, with the disappearance of these late veterans who have done their last "turn" and made their final exit, the old School of Minstrelsy is, indeed, become but a memory.

True, perhaps, a few still linger, but they have gone way back and sat down; their ancient jokes and witticisms have paled and amuse no more, their voices as silent as their departed brothers, forgotten, crowded off the stage by fickle, capricious, ever-changing fashion, "has beens," dead to the present generation—alas! poor Yoricks, only to be recalled by their obituaries! Certainly death has been busy of late, and has gathered a rich harvest—Billy Emerson, the prince of song and dance artists; you should have heard him in "I'm just as Happy as a Big Sunflower," or "Pretty as a Picture," though it was Mme. Aimee, the Opera Bouffe Prima Donna, who Jim Fiske, when a manager, imported from France, and who really popularized the latter, which was composed by Brigham Bishop and laid on the shelves in the music stores for several years before she discovered it, sang it, and it soon became the rage. And Billy Rice and Billy West, "Taken." Artists they were if ever there were any on the minstrel stage. And last, though he was not a minstrel comedian, yet one most prominently identified with minstrels' palmy days, round whose name clusters the memories of the past, genial Neil Bryant, the last of the Bryant brothers.

Dan, Jerry and Neil—and reminiscent of the now long silent Bryant's Minstrels, who for about ten years held sway as the most popular minstrel company in New York, and whose cozy little hall at 472 Broadway was a veritable mint. Often their yearly profits reached $40,000; but the brothers were high livers, and so their estates were easily administered.

In 1875, Dan Bryant made his last bow to the public, and only Neil was left. He reorganized the old company, but with Dan and Jerry gone the *esprit de corps* was lacking, and the fickle public looked elsewhere for amusement.

Neil's specialty was the flutina, and how he could play it! His solo on that instrument was always a most pleasing feature of the bill. He toured to some extent with his reorganized company, but the magic of the name had gone, and the life of the company was brief. After that he appeared on several vaudeville stages, finally abandoning his professional life in 1883. His later years were spent in a clerkship in the Coast Survey Department in Washington. He died in St. Mary's Hospital, Brooklyn, after a very protracted illness.

With the termination of Bryant's Minstrels, the advent of the Lydia Thompson school of burlesque, and the "Bob" Butler class of varieties, minstrelsy may be said to have commenced to wane, and soon the old-time minstrel performance was driven from the stage.

Rather a sad reflection, isn't it? But the "world do move," and were those who have "crossed the divide" to return they'd hardly find a footing. I sometimes wonder would old T. D. Rice, in his "Jump, Jim Crow," which made him famous the world over, be even tolerated today; or the first darkey burlesque opera, "Oh, Hush!" delight the audiences with its pretty, characteristic melodies, as in days of yore. And the performers were true delineators, too, and irresistibly droll. A verse of one of their seriously-ludicrous songs describing their fear of the watchman ran as follows:

"Dat's de same ole watchman dat we have been a-foolin', jolly my lingo lay; so cut your sticks, you darkies, an' I'll meet you in de mornin', jolly my lingo lay." I wonder if the little musical and terpsichorean sketch of the coquettish Lucy Long, its female impersonator and flirtation scene with the handkerchief would occasion the delight it once did. Shades of Leon, Rice, Eugene, Tommy Peel, your vocation's gone! And the "Essence of Ole Virginny," a real piece of acting, that made Frank Brower (who created the dance), Dan Bryant, Ben Cotton, Billy Arlington, Mert Sexton and a few others famous. I used to play the dance for Frank Brewer at Henry Wood's minstrels, on Broadway, and on every occasion with renewed pleasure. I always enjoyed it, and so did our audiences. And the old-time walkarounds, introducing the full force of the company in the liveliest, noisiest and most grotesque dancing and shouting, as each dancer, after circling the stage a few times, would give a vigorous dance, terminating with an attitude or a most emphatic bringing down of the foot. The walkaround invariably concluded the performance, in fact was deemed the only fitting termination, and always dismissed the audience in a satisfied and delighted mood. I wonder would the old time minstrel show meet with equal favor now; and what a revelation to the present generation! I sometimes feel that it would—–—that a revival of real old-time minstrelsy, with its old-time "first part," dress suits, pompous "middle man," a bare quartet of singers, first and second violins, a double bass, perhaps a guitar, a jaw-bone player, who rattled over the teeth with a rib bone; a triangle player, and a "bones" and a'"tambo" artist with their outrageously big pointed paper collars, and exercising their jokes and conundrums on the ends. Somehow there seemed a home-like pleasure and innocence in those old-time entertainments which I miss in those of to-day. But it's human nature I suppose—nothing quite equals our early days recollections.

But surely those were the days when our composers created some of their sweetest lays, their most melodious minstrel melodies and songs—"Old Folks at Home," "Nelly Was a Lady," "Suwanee River," "Massa's in De Cold, Cold Ground," "Old Uncle Ned," "Old Dog Tray," "We Are Coming, Sister Mary," "Old Kentucky Home"—songs which still live, whose pathos and sweetness still touch the heart in sweet echoes of the past, and which will never cease. They don't write such songs nowadays. Conditions are changed. And then, no performance was complete without a banjo solo; not always artistic or instrumental—only rarely so, as "virtuosos" were scarce then—but comic and in plantation dress, a few "remarks," a local ditty, with hits on the times, or some of the "standards'—"Old Hard Times," "Wake Up Skillet," "Jordan Am a Hard Road to Trabbel," "Old Joe," "Keemo Kimo" etc. And a jig dancer? Indispensable ! A good, straight. clean jig there must be, and there *were* jig dancers then:

John Diamond, Lew Rattler, Jack Huntley, Mitchell, Juba, most remarkable colored dancer, who could execute a dance on a bushel measure, and Master Barney, who sought to rival the exquisite dresser and dancer, Tommy Peel, who danced a match for a silver champion belt at the old Broome Street Theatre, corner of Broome and Broadway, with Dick Carroll, an aspirant for the championship. What a crowd it drew! House packed that afternoon. Betting ran high, for both had hosts of friends. I well remember it, for I played for Tommy, taking on two banjos to guard against a broken string. Tommy won the belt. The judge on that occasion was the old comedian, Bob Hart, who a few years ago, and after he had become a preacher, got into a rather serious trouble, fell from grace, and found release from earthly cares through morphine.

So wags the world. And what a host of minstrels has passed over to the majority! Vale! They performed well their mission and are they all forgotten? Most of them. But I know one person who has done much to preserve their names from obscurity, and it is but justice to laud him for his grand work.

There is a restaurant at 126 Greenwich Avenue, opposite Jackson Square, New York City, which has been kept by its present proprietor, Charles H. Britting, for the past thirty years, and has become well known as "The Professional Hall of Fame." This may cause some surprise to those who have never visited the place, and I would advise those who are ignorant of its existence, and would desire to revive old memories of the professional world, to visit the hall, where I can assure them of meeting with a most cordial welcome from its genial and most obliging proprietor. Mr. Britting, of German extraction, is endowed with a modest, quick, quaint wit, which puts his visitors in good humor and at ease at once. His estimable wife, who shares the responsibilities of the establishment, is the counterpart of her husband in amiability and hospitality. Mr. Britting enjoys a world-wide reputation as an antiquarian, a pursuit he has followed out of pure love and enthusiasm for professionals, for he has limited his acquisitions mainly to this specialty. In his early youth he evinced a fondness for the stage, and at the age of fifteen appeared often in amateur theatricals and concerts, and became expert as an accordionist.

His amiable helpmeet, richly endowed with a rare musical faculty, is possessed of a highly cultivated voice that for musical expression, richness and purity will compare favorably with many of our most gifted professional singers, and had she chosen a professional career would have gained prominence for herself in the ranks of our most favored celebrities. But, as with her husband, her ambition finds full gratification in the peace and pleasures of private life and the association of her host of friends.

It seems a pity that neither developed the musical abilities with which they were so richly endowed. But fate willed it otherwise.

Their "Professional Hall of Fame" is plain and unassuming in external appearance, but has more individuality probably than any other restaurant anywhere. The passer-by might see in the window a few quaint old show bills, with pictures of actors in old-time costumes, but nothing about the place could arouse his curiosity unless he chanced to get a glimpse through the door of walls literally covered with old-fashioned play bills.

Mr. Britting is one of the rarest personalities, and is the antiquarian *par excellence* of the professional world. His collection of play bills exceeds 10,000. But this is but an item of the treasures his hall contains. He has amusement literature of every description, programmes from the earliest days to date, posters, hangers, pictures, newspaper files, descriptive articles, amusement notes, events in the world of amusements, obituaries of the men and women who have had their day and have passed to the silent majority; letters, pictures, photos, lithos; in fact, every scrap of anything pertaining in any way to what is known as "show" and professional business, covering every form of public entertainment, not alone of the United States, but foreign countries, as well, until he has accumulated undoubtedly the largest, rarest, most varied, extensive and oldest collection of its kind in the world.

Mr. Britting's collections, aside from their curio features, are invaluable for reference. His newspaper files are simply prodigious. His *New York Clipper* file is complete from its first issue to date. He is the lessee of two adjoining houses, and the lower floors are perfect warehouses of these antique curiosities. In the minstrel line alone he has programs from the dawn of minstrelsy to the present time. Covering the walls from ceiling to floor are four rows of frames containing old programs, photographs and lithographs of famous professionals. But to attempt a full description of this wonderful place is useless. All I can say is — visit it, and you'll be well repaid.

I regret that want of space forbids more than this meagre description of "The Professional Hall of Fame," but cannot conclude without advising all professionally inclined, and all who would gratify a curiosity for a glimpse of the professional world to visit this notable place, where I know, from personal experience, they would - they will be — most cordially welcomed by mine host and hostess, the professionals' friends, Mr. and Mrs. Charles H. Britting.

Banjo Reminiscences. XIV

Written Exclusively for 'THE CADENZA. July, 1902
BY FRANK B. CONVERSE, NEW YORK CITY.

How artistic! What remarkable execution! I never ...
Ah, but wait, my dear friend; you don't seem to
understand. You are mistaken. That's not banjo
playing. It may look like it, sound something like it,
but no, it's not banjo playing. You, doubtless, are not
aware of it, but the truth is, he is not versed in the
theoretical principles of harmony, thorough bass,
counterpoint, etc. — really has but a smattering of
musical ideas. Somewhat of a genius, quite a novel
performance, I may allow, but artistic? A player? Far
from it, my dear fellow, I assure you.

Oh, yes! I see! That's different. I wasn't aware. Not
so artistic or remarkable as I thought. Ha, ha; thanks,
awfully. This is but a little conversation suggested
after reading a very lengthy criticism on the
respective abilities of banjo players and what
constituted a player, recently published in the *New
York Sun.*

Now, it is not my intention to engage in a criticism of the aforementioned criticism—if it may be called such—believing it an open privilege for anyone to revel in the iridescent lines of their own subjectivity and enjoy any satisfaction to be derived from the consciousness of feeling that they are the greatest thing that ever happened; but I cannot refrain from indulging in a few remarks.

My first wonder, upon reading the article, was that so much of the kind could be thought out on the topic; and then it occurred to me that a critic, to be entitled to any consideration, should be well known for his efficiency. But then, in the multifariousness of human nature, it is easy to believe that there are some individuals who, quite undismayed, readily seize upon an opportunity to entangle themselves in most any question in the belief that pure criticism consists chiefly of vituperative expletives, odious comparisons or condemnation on general principles, comforting themselves with the reflection: I criticize, therefore I am a critic; and so, for the instant, feel an exaltation above their victims, quite oblivious of the fact that a pretty thorough knowledge of the subject is a valuable prerequisite. However, to comment is anybody's privilege; but to criticize, to assert, needs facts.

And how stand the facts in the criticism to which I have referred as they relate to Mr. Ruby Brooks and others whom I might mention? Quoting from the article: "But his narrow-minded progeny" (speaking of the "elder Dobson," who never was connected with Brooks, nor with many others), "along with many other well-known banjoists of the old school, notably such men as Ruby Brooks and his young partner Denton and their numerous followers all over the country during the last decade, have done all in their power through ignorance, professional prejudices, and an utter lack in their mental make-up of any musical conception whatever, to make the banjo despised by musicians and ridiculed by the cultivated public, thereby bringing about their own ruin."

Our critic would not for a moment "accuse these men of insincerity," for, as he says, "I know they love the banjo and the noise they made out of it," and that the greater resemblance their playing bears to a chorus of Gatling guns in full action the more they are pleased with themselves." And further — "They cannot find words mean enough to express their utter contempt for the first men that brought a note of music from the strings of a banjo." Well, bringing a "note" from a string is all right, I suppose, as a mild personification—but we are more accustomed to seeing them on the staff. However, that's a small matter. But it must occasion general surprise to be informed that the banjo "sprang from some crude form of instrument made by barbarians," which solves the mystery heretofore enveloping the germ banjo, and will disabuse the minds of those who fondly, but ignorantly cherished the hope that it came from the realm of the angels.

How learnedly our critic discusses the virtues of the banjo that we shall be properly and conclusively enlightened. He says: "The difference between the banjo's musical virtues and those of other modern instruments is simply in its comparative age." Further particulars are lacking, but probably he takes it for granted that his readers will take his assertion for granted, which is an apparent assumption throughout the article. Yet it would be interesting to know at what period of time the germ banjo really commenced its evolution. But it is a measure of relief to learn that the banjo possesses virtues other than its Gatling gun propensities, which, after all, may be but a youthful ebullition of spirit when we are made to know that "the banjo is in its infancy." However, we need not take this weakness too seriously; the instrument is to outgrow its infantile whims and be preserved from what might have been its oblivion by "men of marked musical talent who have preferred to attempt the development of the banjo, and have succeeded both musically and monetarily," which is "evidence enough that instead of passing into oblivion the banjo's day is but just dawning." Glorious! All hail the coming dawn!

But here we have it,—a discovery that *is* a discovery, "touchin' on an' appertainin' to" the subject, as expressed in polite parlance: "But the primary secret of success with the banjo, as with every other stringed instrument, is touch." Touch not, handle not, is hardly understood to apply to a musical instrument, but to many obtuse minds I think the inference our learned critic would make apparent, that the banjo has heretofore remained untouched — which ordinarily would seem bordering upon the incredible, is yet not to be taken too literally; but that it received its first real soothing touch from the dimpled fingers of a most modern, up-to-date infant! Ah, not only out of mouths of babes but in their finger-tips are we in this age to be indebted for knowledge!

But, gentlemen, remember that facts are stubborn things. And don't our critic enlighten us when he tells us that "One instance will serve as an example to show in a general way how the new school banjoist came about. A child of about 11 years of age had a sudden whimsical desire to possess a banjo. His parents gratified his desire and he set to work with a will and an obsolete Winner instruction book to master the instrument. He soon began to complain of the tone of the banjo — this precocious infant! — "it did not sound at all like a banjo! — this remarkable executant and judge! — "there was no snap to it;" — not a "soft snap" for the infant, evidently.

"But his mother was a musician; after hearing

others play on her son's banjo with all the nasal tone and fire-cracker snap that could possibly be desired—or tolerated—with the quick wit of a practical musician decided it was all a matter of touch and that her son had unwittingly produced the true tone of the instrument." There you have it, gentlemen. You can now understand how the thing came about. And the infant first touched the banjo, whose sweetness, imminent but inert, lay slumbering, awaiting the soul—revivifying contact. The boy had it, you see. Simple enough when you arc told of it. The boy formed the circuit ; found the lost, no, I mean the never-before-discovered touch. That's it. Touching, isn't it?

Our critic does not stop here but gives us an analysis of this remarkable event which will be properly appreciated by all who may have been touched by this almost pathetic tale. He says: "The old-style banjoist plays with his fingers curved like hooks, so that when he strikes a string the end of his finger goes under it and he picks it with an upward motion and lets it snap back, thus cutting the vibrations short against the head."

Of course all new banjoists will now strive to avoid "cutting" the vibrations, and not allow 'the strings to strike the head of the banjo. Heretofore, the bridge has been quite useful in preventing the strings from contact with the drum: but then it's well to know don't you know?

But this is not all. He desires that you shall "get onto the touch. So he tells us "To acquire a proper touch the strings must be struck with straight fingers." Gentleman banjoists, have you ever tried to execute this feat? Try it. Yet I fear it will trouble some of you back-of-date players to learn that, as he most pleasingly says the result will be a pure, open tone that in the upper notes will be as sweet as that of the harp, but a trifle sharper, giving them a bell-like quality, while the lower notes are full and rich, but entirely unique. 'Unique' is good, refreshing, encouraging. We now have the secret of touch. Straight fingers will do the business, and bell tones, harp tones, full tones, rich tones will peal forth to delight and intoxicate the soul of the newly inspired and modified banjoist. Eureka! banjoists, straighten your fingers! But enough of this. Sufficient, I think, has been quoted to convince our gatling gunners that they can no longer impose their firecracker explosives on a too long ignorant and indulging public.

But really, and getting down to common sense, how comes it that, all of a sudden, as it were, Brooks is discovered to be not a banjoist?

Certainly the gentleman has for a long series of years posed as one, and if not a player, his case exhibits one of the most remarkable and successful impositions ever perpetrated upon a musical public.

To be sure, he has utterly failed to execute with "straight" fingers, but in view of his really phenomenal, unwavering success, here and abroad, I believe we ought charitably to be willing to overlook the defect(?).

Mr. Brooks, it might almost be said, may be ranked with the old-time banjoists, for he has been before the public for many years, not only as a professional stage player, but a teacher as well; and his pupils run up into the thousands. Think of the thousands of Gatling gunners he has produced! His public playing has been a prominent feature in concerts and entertainments the world over, playing in conjunction with the most eminent artists of the musical profession, and he has always been the recipient of the most flattering encomiums in the comments of the press.

The following criticism from the *Newburgh Daily News*, Oct. 12. 1887, is but a repetition in substance of the thousands gathered in England and America. "The talent of Mr. Brooks has become well known in this city. His wonderful execution, the clear, pure tones he produces, and the high-class music he renders on his instrument are really marvelous."

A Boston paper, reviewing his career, states: "Mr. Brooks remarkable playing has secured for him the first prize at all the leading banjo tournaments in New York City, Boston, and elsewhere."

He has taught royalty, and many of the most eminent personages in England, and has had the honor of playing before the Prince (King Edward) and Princess of Wales at Marlborough House, Lady Paget, Duchess of Fife, Lady Randolph Churchill, Lady Sullivan, Duke of Edinburgh, Lady Cooke, and nobility and royalty *ad infinitum*. Just imagine how he has worked his imposition on all these people. People who are really considered musical, and competent judges! Monstrous! The musical world is to be pitied for such dense ignorance. 'Way back in the early 80's Mr. Brooks was publicly written of as "an artist in showing the banjo's right to rank with the violin, the piano, or harp, and developing such musical method and mastery in playing it as to win for himself the title of a virtuoso." He was even then playing such selections as "La Gitana," "The Funeral March of a Marionette," Arditi's famous "Gavotte," "Tannhäuser," overtures to operas, classical selections and other intricate numbers, to the marvel of musicians who were delighted at his fidelity in execution.

But really, I think one might be better employed than in enumerating the exploits of "one of the narrow minded progeny" who has, our critic asserts, done SO much "to make the banjo despised by musicians and ridiculed by the cultivated public, thereby bringing about their own ruin." Of course, the aforementioned criticism takes Mr. Brooks' measure, that he is not a banjoist—only a cunning impostor. But I boldly take an exception to the assertion that he has brought about his own ruin, to substantiate which it is only necessary to refer to the more than successful publishing and teaching firm of Brooks & Denton, now, and for many years, located at 670 Sixth Avenue, New York City, where evidences of prosperity will be found sufficient to most completely dispel any such absurd delusion. And now a few words about Mr. Brooks partner, Mr. Denton, and this will be best accomplished by copying from his recent letter to me requesting data relating to himself. He says:

"I hardly know how to reply to your request. As for myself, I was born on Long Island, Jan. 25, 1865. When I was 8 years old my father bought me a $2 banjo on Grand Street, New York.

"I remember receiving a few lessons from a person named Frank Benner. He advised my parents to have me 'stick to it,' and this, I believe, I have done. About 1880 I met Antonio Bini, the guitarist. I was very much taken with the guitar, and worked very hard at it with him for a few years. In 1887 I first met Mr. Brooks when on my way to a rehearsal with some mandolin players. He told me of a banjo tournament which was to take place on May 10 at Chickering Hall, and persuaded me to enter. He loaned me a banjo and I rehearsed for a few days in the old Park Theatre (now the Herald Square) with Mr. Frank Weber, now deceased, a wonderfully fine piano accompanist for the banjo. The contest, open to all, took place, about a dozen or fifteen participating, including Ossman, Doré, Emerson, Eckland and others I cannot now recall. The judges were A. D. Cammeyer (now of London, Eng.), James Winslow, New York; Gad Robinson, Boston, and Dunbar Wright, New York. To my surprise I took the second prize, Mr. Brooks taking the first prize.

"We then formed our partnership and opened at our present address in September, 1887. We have since given annual concerts in the city, the feature of which being the first gathering of 100 banjos in concert. I was the leader, — that is, it looked so, but before the first strain I found them leading me. However, the effect pleased and the concerts were decided successes. We repeated them for several successive years. We gave Volfé, the mandolinist his opening in New York, likewise Romero, guitarist Siegel, mandolinist; Farland, banjoist, twice ; and the autocratic banjoist, Miss Fanny Heinline.

"I believe Mr. Brooks rendition of Moszkowski's Spanish dance and our selections from "Tannhauser" were the first attempt at anything serious on the banjo. Then some of the papers and would-be critics ridiculed the idea, but a change has come over them. Our engagements now are all private and for select functions only. We had the honor of playing for Prince Henry at the luncheon at Sherry's, Feb. 26th. On March 7th, when the University Club asked the Prince what sort of music he wished at their dinner, he replied that he wished the same as at Sherry's, so we were selected for the event.

"The study of music is a constant and pleasing one with me. Mr. Brooks' busy teaching engagements are a constant course of education in music, but we have little time to go further than the practical part of it.

"We arrange quite extensively for the different music publishers, all grades of desirable music, and it is gratifying to know that our arrangements are found satisfactory. As to our business in general, well, we are always busy, yet can always spare a few moments to greet our friends."

Banjo Reminiscences. XV

Written Exclusively for THE CADENZA. September, 1902
BY FRANK B. CONVERSE, NEW YORK CITY.

After an absence of several years, "working" a distant "circuit," William—No !— "Billy"! Arlington returns to New York, confessing that there's no place like it, except Chicago, Saint Louis, Minneapolis, and a few other cities of the great West—for a while! And he should *know*, for he *has* traveled; been "on the road," as a showman would say, ever since his "boyhood's happy days," and that's stating a pretty long stretch of years; but his infancy was nearly contemporary with that of minstrelsy with which he grew and has grown throughout its varied metamorphoses, and to its very bier! But he is innocent of its demise, for a more studious, earnest aider and abettor of the art de Ethiopic never "assumed the sable," nor stood sponsor or preceptor for more of its followers who, under his tutelage have made their mark in black, some later attaining prominence in other professional walks, while many, though not forgotten, have "passed over" to the "great aggregate."

It was with "Billy" Arlington that Francis Wilson, of comic opera fame, received his first professional impulse—and through burnt cork. And John Wild, who became famous as a black comedian and comic banjoist, and who eventually retired to a farm he had purchased upon terminating his professional career with Harrigan and Hart, who also were with Mr. Arlington in their early days. And Leon—"the only Leon," who became the black Prima Donna par *excellence*, with but few peers, notably William Henry Rice, Frank Kent, Chas. Heywood, and Eugene.

Eugene died in England where he had long associated with Unsworth, the banjoist and comedian. Rice and others still remain, actively attached to their early love. Leon (but that's not his name) is now a prosperous landlord in a Western city.

And there was Billy Emerson, Bobby Newcomb, Cool Burgers, Frank Dumont, now manager of the Eleventh Street Opera House, Philadelphia, Carncross and Dixies, Billy Rice, and many other notables who might be named, under his management at times. As an all-around performer, "Billy" Arlington's versatility seems limitless. His readiness in emergency was well illustrated on one occasion when, being "called" for his banjo solo, and discovering that his instrument was broken, he caught up a broom, which he substituted, and with the orchestra accompanying, made, as he says, "the hit of his life." It is needless to say he added the act to his repertoire.

As a comic banjoist he ranks with Billy Carter and that's praise enough — both artists in this specialty, though differing in style; and it has aided their success that neither ever aspired to become virtuosos; realizing, I believe, that sufficient for the act was their banjoic attainments thereof.

As a violinist, there *may* have been worse, but the knowledge of this fact did not deter him from assuming '1st" in an early company with which he engaged.

As a dancer, he was one of the few successful followers of Frank Brower in the latter's famous dance—"Essence of Old Virginny." Inspired by the "Essence," he conceived the idea of a similar dance in petticoats and his "Mississippi Fling," extravagantly characteristic, took his audiences by storm.

As a comic lecturer, wit, mimic and entertainer he has but few peers and the jokes and stories for which he is responsible have supplied material which has gained popularity for many an aspiring professional. If written they would fill a large book. To have created 'Uncle Ephraim's Lectures," and "Rastus on the Watermelon Question" should be fame enough.

As proprietor and manager, aside from individual enterprises he has associated at various times with such prominent professionals as John Donniker, Kelly and Leon, Sam Meyers, Ben Cotton, W. W. Newcomb, M. B. Leavitt, in California, etc. I had an established company in Chicago in 1863, built the Academy of Music, which he conducted for several years, and has employed most of the best known performers in the profession. After the Chicago fire (1876) he organized Arlington, Cotton and Kemble's minstrels and erected the well-known Meyers' Opera House.

Referring to his early experience, he said: "I was born young" (seemingly a little reticent on this point), 'way up in York State. At the age of five my parents moved to New York and, owing to our close relationship, I was easily induced to accompany them. When but a little 'shaver' I scraped enough money together to purchase a fiddle from a barber and, having no more cash, became my own teacher. I took to it quite naturally and soon the fiddle and I became of some consequence at little parties, picnics and such. Seeing an advertisement in the *Herald* for musicians, and believing I was one, I applied for the position of leader and was accepted.

"This may surprise you, but it wasn't to be a very strong company. All told it numbered five, and that included a trick dog I borrowed from my brother when he was away. Our 'route' was up the Hudson River. I was to play the fiddle, tell Yankee stories and perform the dog—the only artist in the company. As the audiences we looked for failed to respond to our little handbills, things came to a crisis which completed our 'circuit' in just four days, leaving each to his own resources. So we re-organized, that is, Oscar Searles, our banjoist, myself and the dog formed a new combination. Fortunately our baggage was light and easily disposed of in the banjo bag. With my fiddle carefully wrapped in a portable newspaper we started out to raid the nearby towns, preferring to walk than endanger the lives of the new combination. Thus we traveled from town to town until the dog having become lame and Searles's banjo broken, we decided to close the season, mutually congratulating that we had escaped with our lives. With the little money I had succeeded in hoarding I bought Searles' banjo and returned to my home. Laying aside the fiddle, I took up the banjo, with which I was better pleased, and when I had mastered a few jigs and could accompany my songs, I was again open for dates.

"At that time (1858), William Hitchcock was running an English chop house on Canal Street, near the Bowery and had constructed a "Music Hall" in the rear; a sort of fenced-in place with a canvas cover. Here, in company with Jerry Merrifield (a comedian) and Miss Celia Morley, a pianist I played my first engagement; and was well satisfied, though my salary was but eight dollars, that I remained for several months. A better salary led me to the Melodeon on Broadway, managed by Frank River. In 1859, "Pic" Butler, the banjoist "Jimmy" Clark, another, Frank Wells and myself engaged to do our specialties with Avery Smith and Quick, the circus managers, for Havana, Cuba, where we were well received. One of the oddities was that during intermissions the audience, men and women, would visit us in our dressing rooms. Returning from Havana, I was engaged by George H. Christy, then playing a company at Niblo's saloon, Broadway, as end man and general comedian, and I wouldn't have exchanged places with the President of the United States. I traveled with this company throughout the States. This was just preceding the Civil War. When at Charleston, South Carolina, the people were holding secret secession meetings and there was great excitement. A grand banquet was given in honor of Jefferson Davis, Gen. Robert E. Lee, Beauregard and other noted Southerners, and our company was honored with an invitation. It was a grand affair; the speechifying was hot, a magnificent spread, and wine flowed like water. We played a week to packed houses, and my banjo song, "But you can't never wash a nigger white," local for the occasion, created tremendous fervor. The house went wild; even the ladies rising and waving their handkerchiefs in applause. The sentiment of the song struck a responsive chord. From Charleston we played all through the South to New Orleans; then up the Mississippi to St. Louis when Fort Sumter was fired upon, which closed the South to us, and you know the sequel."

Sorry that space forbids following my subject farther. However, I think I have written enough to confirm the inference that "Billy" is a veteran. But one wouldn't believe it to see him — the wear and tear you'd expect to see are lacking. Doubtless as reward for steady habits and a genial disposition, Time has touched him lightly, and his "sands of life" seem far from running out! And though the minstrel field has been ploughed and furrowed by many inroads and so no longer affords a pasturage, his occupation's not gone; for there remain other fields, fresh and fertile, wherein his genius may glean, with opportunities strict minstrelsy prescribed, and free from the jealousies so frequently engendered by rivalry in companies. For now he's the whole thing itself — his own entire company from baggage hustler to manager and all through the bill, as the following sample program will attest:

i.   Mr. Arlington's premier presentation of his
       Protean Characterizations entitled
       THE RAILROAD MEETING.:
       CHARACTERS IMPERSONATED.
       The President
       Mr. Snipe
       Mr. Fairplay
       Mrs. Fidgett
       Mr. Blunt
       Mr. Perkins
       Mr. Snapshot
       Mr. Snivel
       Mr. Smallback

ii.
       Place: The Town Hall.
       OBJ ECT OF THE MEETING : 'The
       Suppression of Newspapers and Railroads."
       2. Deacon Bradshaw's Sermon: Text — "Old

Mother Hubbard."

3. Burlesque Lecture on Female Suffrage" —
— Impersonating Susan B. Anthony.

4. A Bit of Pathos : "A God After All."

5. Banjo Song — Burlesque : "Home Sweet
Home."

6. Minstrel Jokes.

7. Song — With Banjo: "Old Uncle Ned"
— Old and new versions.

8. A Touch of Nature : "A Tribute to
Mother."

9. Story: "My Brother."

10. Banjo Song: "The Dear Old Rooster"
— With exact imitations of all kinds of
crowing roosters.

ii. Minstrel Jokes.

12 . Story: "The Englishman, The Irishman
and The Scotchman."

13. Topical Speech: "Labor versus Capital.

14. Banjo Song: "The Pumpkin Pies My
Mother Used to Make."

15. Minstrel Jokes.

16. Alphabet Story of the Spanish-American
War.

17. A Bit of Humor: "How to Travel Without
R. R. Fare."

18. Plantation Pleasantry: "Uncle Ephraim
Lectures Rastus on the Watermilyun
Question."

19. Juvenile Recitation: "Seem' Things" —
byEugene Field.

20. A Tribute to Odd Fellowship.
21. Song: "Mary's Gone Wid a Coon" — An imitation of an old plantation darkey.
22. Poem: "Only a Dog."

Printed in Great Britain
by Amazon.co.uk, Ltd.,
Marston Gate.